Belt and Road Initiative of the Maritime Silk Road Confucius Institute

Phraprommangkalachan, Ed.D.

ISBN-13:978-1979455183
ISBN-10:197945518X

Maritime Silk Road Confucius Institute
海上丝路孔子学院

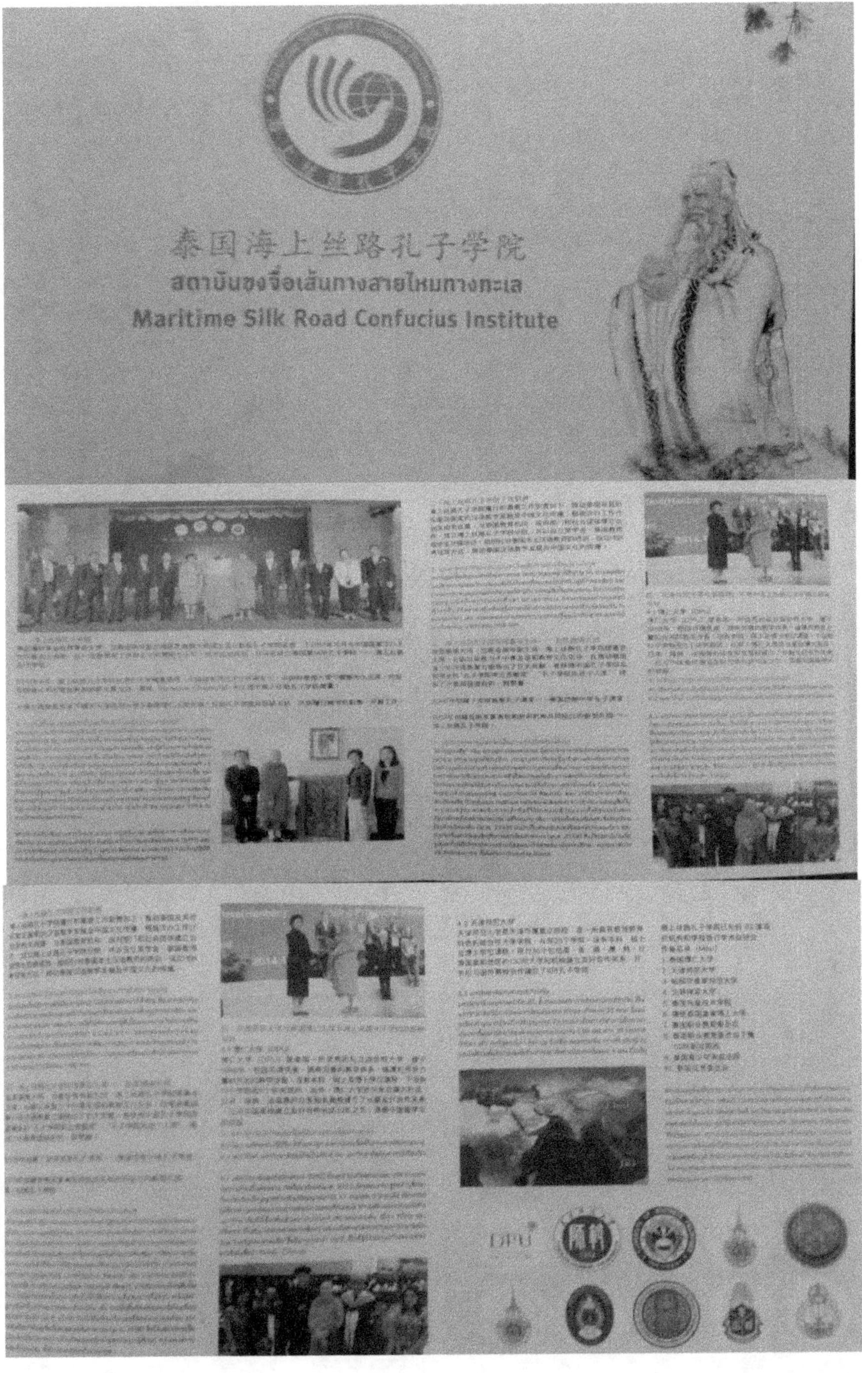
泰国海上丝路孔子学院
สถาบันขงจื๊อเส้นทางสายไหมทางทะเล
Maritime Silk Road Confucius Institute

DEDICATION

The Maritime Silk Road Confucius Institute has been the forefront of the
providing world peace and development in the Asian region
through cultural academic exchange program, political and economic
diplomacy to create the idealism of amity and comity
among the sovereign states.

The Maritime Silk Road has been there as part of the economic, political
and cultural activities of the Asian people for many centuries
that need to be revived again not only for the sake of knowing it
but the essence of consciousness which transcends
what is moral and right in the quest of *nirvana* that revolves within center of
heart and soul of the human society.

The essence of "Belt and Road Initiative" demands the full dedication of
humanity to open their minds to understand the bright side in a long dark
tunnel   of mistrust by world leaders.
The openness diversifies the image of human compassion dictated by trust
and confidence to live in harmony of love and peace among nations.
The constructive bipolar view of closeness defines the oneness of spirits
when entangled with trust the world will shower us
the flowers of good deeds among men never seen even birth of the
Maritime Silk Road that economically and politically built by our
forefathers.

Let this book continuously inspire us to settle our differences on what we
think that is good for us not for others.
We think so much about world dominations based on our political interests
and ideologies that we never thought that destroyed the very essence
of what we are in this world.
The existence of humanity must be cherished by what we had done in the
past like the presence of the Maritime Silk Road
that brought us together as " One Asian nation" with our allies on the
other sphere of influence as we deal them of peaceful diplomacy.

Let this book be dedicated to all of us to bring the greater glory on
"Oneness , Openness and Closeness" that synthesize our ideal academic
understanding of the " Belt and Road Initiative" within the loyal
commitment of the Maritime Silk Rod Confucius Institute...

CONTENTS

ACKNOWLEDGMENTS

This fourth book entitled "**Belt and Road Initiative of the Maritime Silk Road Confucius**" is the expanded version of the " **One Belt One Road Initiative: Universal Perspectives in World Peace and Development through Change, Innovation, Idealism and Freedom**" to further establish the presence of the Maritime Silk Road Confucius Institute in the promotion of cultural diversity, economic and political diplomacy in the Asian region . The Romchatra Foundation and Hanban with the participation of ASEAN foreign universities and the institute (Maritime Silk Road Confucius Institute at Dhurakij Pundit University) for continuously supporting the academic publications to promote the essence of oneness and closeness of the Asian people. It will also develop and forge independent foreign policy within the ideal view of comity and amity that will ensure world peace and development in the sovereign states that will participate the "Belt and Road Initiative" through the Maritime Silk Road in Asian region.

The establishment of the Maritime Silk Road Confucius Institute acknowledges the Hanban of the Chinese government through the support of the Confucius Institute Headquarters. The Chinese leadership of President Xi Jinping has been able to provide the new paradigm shift of the "Belt and Road Initiative" in the development of political, cultural and economic philosophy in the modern world. In the point of view of political and economic philosophy, it defines so much about diplomatic peaceful coexistence bounded by mutual respect, non-interference and non-aggression in the territorial integrity of sovereign states. The joint economic ventures and infrastructure development in the "Belt and Road Initiative" of President Xi Jinping empowered the rest of the Asian community to restore the social gaps that will bring closer to the fulfillment of the improved quality of life because of the employment generation , high income compensation, and investment opportunities to create a decent life for all humanity in the Asian countries.

The prime mover of the Chinese educational and cultural programs provided by Madam Xu Lin, Chief Executive of Confucius Institute Headquarters and Director General of Hanban with the, Chinese Ambassador to Thailand, Varakorn Samakoses. Those who participated in the launching program of the Maritime Silk Road Confucius Institute were the following : Deputy Minister of the Ministry of Education in Thailand, Ning Fukui, Chinese Ambassador to Thailand, Varakorn Samakoses, President of Dhurakij Pundit University and Zhong Yinghua, Vice President of Tianjin Normal University. Furthermore, the author would like to acknowledge the heartfelt dedication, support and commitment of the following Board Members of Maritime Silk Confucius Institute: Dr. Xu Lin, Director General of Hanban (Vice Minister); Dr, Zhou Gaoyu, Director of Education Office (First Secretary); Dr. Nilubol Limpongpan; Mrs. Pranee Sungkatavat; Mr. Poonsak Pranootnaraparn; Mr. Varakorn Samakoses; Mrs. Arunee Juktreemongkol; and Mr. Jang Yang.

Furthermore, this is to acknowledge the support and guidance of all the Board Directors and Affiliate Members of the Maritime Silk Road Confucius Institute for painstakingly providing the sustained academic activities in foreign universities, government offices and other entities to implement the development goals of the "Belt and Road Initiative" in the Asian countries. The best practices promulgated by the Maritime Silk Road Confucius included the Chinese Language Competition through the Diamond on the Top Crown project.

The Board of Directors of Maritime Silk Road Confucius Institute are as follows

1.	Phraprommangkalachan	President
2.	Dr. Sathit Limpongpan	Vice President
3.	Associate professor Dr. Varakorn Samakoses	Vice President
4.	General Pinpart Sariwat	Board of Director
5.	Police Lieutenant General ML. Punsak Kasemsan	Board of Director
6.	Associate Professor Dr. Pranee Sangkhasap	Board of Director
7.	Associate Professor Dr. Chuangchot Pantuweat	Board of Director
8.	Associate Professor Dr. Issaree hunsacharoonroj	Board of Director
9.	Dr. Nilubol Limpongpan	Board of Director
10.	Dr. Darika Lathapipat	Board of Director
11.	Dr. Akanit Kangsang	Board of Director
12.	Mr. Wanchai Sornsiri	Board of Director
13.	Mr. Thanakorn Seriburi	Board of Director
14.	Mr. Niphon Chokphiromwongsa	Board of Director
15.	Mr. Rojana Kritcharoen	Board of Director
16.	Mr. Sansern Ngaorungsi	Board of Director
17.	Mr. Poonsak Pranootnaraparn	Board of Director and Secretary
18.	Mr. Ekarat Janrathitikarn	Board of Director and Deputy Secretary
19.	Mr. He Bingzheng	Board of Director and Deputy Secretary

In the Philippines, the author would like to acknowledge the academic and moral support of the University of Northern Philippines (UNP) in the realization of this project : Dr. Gilbert R. Arce, President, University of Northern Philippines; Dr. Generoso Gudelio P. Pajarillo, Coordinator, Center for International Studies; Dr. Christopher F. Bueno, Dean, College of Teacher Education and the Faculty and Staff of the Graduate Studies for Education. The other academic support of Dr. Khatiyada Chaiyo, UNP Thai Coordinator of the Blended Education Programs (Doctor of Education, Doctor of Business Education and Doctor of Public

Administration) has facilitated the coordination of the Board Members of Maritime Silk Road in the publication of this project.

The University of Northern Philippines through the College of Teacher Education and Graduate Studies for Education has given me the academic reputation and experience in publishing the three (3) books entitled:
1. **One Belt and One Road Initiative : Universal Perspectives in World Peace and Development through Change, Innovation, Idealism and Freedom**
2. **Traimit Educational Model for the First Confucius School in Thailand**
3. **Confucius Institute of Maritime Silk Road: A Diplomatic Strategy for World Peace and Development**

These three (3) books provided the extensive information and knowledge about the educational model of the Chinese culture for the development programs of Maritime Silk Road Confucius Institute in the Asian region. It has also promoted the Chinese language programs of the Confucius Institutes in achieving the win-win approach to fulfil educational peace and prosperity with the diplomatic relations of China-Thailand and other Asian countries. Likewise, the University of Northern Philippines is at the heart of the UNESCO Heritage City of Vigan considered as one of the Seven Wonder Cities in the World that has been promoting the management programs on cultural heritage and diversity propelled from the blending of the east and west influence on buildings, arts, culture including the influence of the Chinese descent in the area.

I further acknowledged those professors who gave me the wisdom to finally put into philosophical writings about my extensive views and ideas in this book on Change, Innovation, Idealism and Freedom beyond the academic contextual view of the Maritime Silk Road. May this book provides genuine knowledge on my inner insights on its transitory continuum ideas for nirvana on Change, Innovation, Idealism and Freedom that will eventually put into minds of our generation for the peaceful actions about the "Belt and Road Initiative" advocated by President Xi Jinping of China.

Phraprommangkalachan, Ed.D.

Chapter I
Essence of Human Life in the Maritime Silk Road : The Philosophical Wisdom of Change, Innovation, Idealism and Freedom

The philosophical wisdom for world peace reflects the simple way to express that "Every day the world turns to break the new day." The element of time embodies the essence of life. This reflects the changing world where the gradual transformation of everyday activities that defines the life cycle of mankind

The lifecycle demands the consciousness of oneself as how we deal the biological clock to live with what something we would like to have in our lifetime. The time element defines what we can do for today and tomorrow as we want to fulfil what we want in life. It must be noted that we live of specific purpose that our self-fulfilment provides us what we need to become in our future. It is the true reflection of the collective endeavours that we must need to fulfil and sustain once we are there. However, the collective material satisfaction denotes of what we want that sometimes cannot be granted overtime.

The material things are given to us by our family, friends and relatives they are the sole derivatives of what we are as they inherited the same with our ancestors. It defines the real purpose of life that has been cared when we cannot exist along where our innocence provides them the compassion and love of what we need. Sometimes, it does matter where we come from whether genetically embodied by our saliva or not. The essence of life depends so much when we grow a seed that too much dependent of what will become as a by-product of love and care.

The existence of life in the essence of time provides us the leeway to reconnect the lived-in experience on a given society. The emotions are automatically entrusted by those who cared and loved us that will influence us by what we become or the environment dictates the tempo our life. However, the essence of life defines what we want to be recognized or appreciated that will inspire our thoughts and emotions of what we become. This is the gradual transformation that every day the world turns to break new day will continue to aspire us on what we want to become from its sense of recognition and appreciation within our egocentrism.

What is given in a society is the natural right to live by the instinct human love which provides us the life support regardless whether this is genetically inclined inception of mind.

However, the most interesting struggle of the life cycle defines by how we govern, how we dictate the kind of goods and services, how we follow our beliefs, ideals and aspirations, and how we weave the knowledge and love we have to live in this beautiful world.

When we discuss the idea of life cycle, it provides the rearing of a family to its development as a clan evolved by collective structural analysis in the existence of a tribe that followed the early civilization of mankind predestined to permanently settled by the river tributaries that existed the fine element of the early development of human society. This was the very reason on the vibrant governance order in the existence of the Maritime Silk Road that inclined to connect each other since the beginning of the early human civilization. In contemporary time, the term "Maritime" defines by the international trade and commerce extended from China sea to the global regions of the world. The Maritime Silk Road had been there throughout the human history that the essentials of life cycle existed by the time element of human civilization.

The human civilization began by the maritime system through the river routes that interconnected by the vast seas and ocean that provided the social interaction and interdependence of the regions of the world. The elders of the tribe were the familial institution of learnings that set generated the cognitive development of human knowledge. The nature's movement and cosmic cycle provided the phenomenological truth as to the rational explanation as to the existence of life. It created the cultural realm dictated by the cosmic forces of nature that became the evolving knowledge and beliefs. The human learnings were attributed by the interpretation and experiences of cosmic knowledge that contributed to the understanding of culture what had known as beliefs, mores, norms, and tradition.

Other than the natural occurrence of the cosmic forces, the maritime system defines the life cycle that existed in the past with various political , and economic activities. The territorial conquest became a part of human activities where the power of barbarism dictated the tempo that shape the geo-political life in all regions of the world. Gradually, the political stability of territorial conquests established ideals of civilized tribes and kingdoms had economic activities that the maritime routes expanded the interdependence of human society.

For many centuries the maritime routes had been the unifying areas of political and economic diplomacy particularly in Asia. The silk became the instrument of peace and development in the continents of Asia, Europe and Africa. This had been done long before the territorial conquest by the European countries to establish the political ideas of expansionism such as Mercantilism, Colonialism and Imperialism. However, the world order of economic development in the east had been well-established what was known as the Maritime Silk Road. The Chinese civilization through the development of the Maritime Silk Road had been instrumental in the economic diplomacy that defined the centuries of peace and development in the regions of Asia.

The revival of the Maritime Silk Road in contemporary time denotes the manifestation of the philosophical wisdom continuously view the human reflections of sufferings and the nirvana of freedom as the centrepiece of cosmic forces of human society. The human life cycle must now come into new economic diplomatic order in the interdependence of states where peace and development existed in the heart and spirit to all of us. We can only do this by the ideals of the Maritime Silk Road where the integration of Confucius Institutes ensure the political, cultural, social and economic diplomacy development advocacies within the realm of INNOVATION, CHANGE, IDEALISM and FREEDOM.

The new day demonstrates the changing perspectives on how we aspire and live our life working harmoniously to attain world peace and development for our future. These are the reflections of the scientific development of society on the ideas of politics that embrace so much of the dichotomy of sufferings and freedom. Consequently, it manifests the considerable struggle of human experience to achieve the new days for innovation, idealism and freedom of a given society.

The blessing for the new day manifests the philosophical wisdom from Phraprommangkalachan (Chaokhun Thongchai) from Traimitwittayaram Voravihan (Temple of the Golden Buddha) consists of (4) four keywords.

1. ***Change:*** *Adapting oneself to suit the new situations, suggesting Suffering (Dukkha).*

2. ***Innovation:*** *Learning and absorbing new cultures, suggesting the Cause of Suffering (Samudaya).*

3. ***Idealism:*** *Holding firm on good faith and creative thinking, suggesting the End of Suffering (Niroda)*

4. ***Freedom:*** *Liberating oneself with wisdom, suggesting the Path Leading to the End of Suffering (Magga)*

These are relevant to the four (4) noble truths of Buddhism which serves as the reflection of the changing of sufferings from its root cause to the cessation of suffering from the idealistic point of view to embrace the change of time and knowledge. The new day is designed to embrace the continuum of time element to reciprocate from the gradual transition from Change on Dukkha where the suffering exists which later on transforms to Innovation on Samudaya and precipitated by the Idealism on Niroda and Freedom on Magga. These are the state of life cycle for the new day transforming gradually the liberation of mind that may later on attain the vision of nirvana.

These are the Four (4) **Noble Truths of Buddhism**

1. **Suffering**. *All existence is unsatisfactory and filled with suffering.*

2. **Cause of Suffering**. *The root of suffering can be defined as an attachment to or craving for wrong things. These desires in the material world can never give us everlasting happiness because by nature they are temporary or transitory.*

3. **End of Suffering**. *By practising right conduct, meditation and prayer it is possible for an individual to attain Liberation or Nirvana.*

4. **Path to the Cessation of Suffering**. *The Noble Eightfold path is the way to finding the solution to suffering and bring it to an end*

Basically, we consider these life cycles of the new day to embrace the development of world peace through change, innovation, idealism and freedom. These are within the clauses of noble truths where Buddhism defines the essence of life from its conception of suffering to the cessation of the gradual path that may follow within the gradual wisdom steps of change, innovation, idealism and freedom.

The next chapter provides the critical transition of the applied philosophy of the ideas of **Change, Innovation, Idealism, and Freedom** to connect the relevance of the " Belt and Road Initiative" as designed in the revival of the Maritime Silk Road Initiative. The development goal of the continuum level of the ideas of **Change, Innovation, Idealism** and **Freedom** reflects the perspective of *Nirvana* that will finally achieve the governance initiative in the improvement of quality of life to all the people of the world.

However, the achievement of *Nirvana* cannot simply come by whatever government actions are doing to achieve the quality of life of those who are affected by the "Belt and Road Initiative" because the sphere of influence in the bipolar world created so much on mistrust and doubt in the true motive in bringing the revival of the Maritime Silk Road for Asia, Africa and Europe. This idea remains the philosophical obstacle from the standpoint of *dukkha* (sufferings) which becomes the hindrance as to acceptability of the sphere of influence for world domination even the genuine gesture in the implementation of the "Belt and Road Initiative" provides all the economic advantage of the sovereign states as the recipients of the universal social and economic welfare programs attributed by the improvement of quality of life for all the people in the world.

Chapter II
Applied Philosophical Overview of the "Belt and Road Initiative" in the Maritime Silk Road

This chapter provides the conceptualization of the applied Philosophy in the implementation of "Belt and Road Initiative" that can be situated in the Maritime Silk Road for Asia, Africa and Europe. It has to discuss the wisdom of nirvana beyond the path of perfection to deal with more meaningful action of the Chinese government that initiated the peaceful transition of diplomatic life in the sovereign states to conform the ideal partnership and collaboration to all continental regions affected by the Maritime Silk Road in the past Asian civilization.

The political ideology does not affect by the intrusion of the concept of "Belt and Road Initiative" by the non-conforming view of western world as to the sincerity about the effect to the diplomatic interest in the sphere influence in the outcome of this program. If tangible development projects are provided by a sovereign state such as the implementation of "Belt and Road Initiative" from its revival of the Maritime Silk Road then the universal obligation of the other sphere of influence should take the candle of light from the political darkness in the consciousness of their minds and hearts from the western world . It had been invented by them the ideas of imperialism, colonialism, mercantilism and absolutism as the dark shadows in the past civilizations and empires.

Bringing Peaceful Transition of the Oriental and Western Philosophy in the Adoption of the "Belt and Road Initiative"

The world existed in the east-west sphere of influence that dictated the human society in the timeline of political, cultural and economic struggles for many centuries. The eastern culture had been well represented by the yellow race where regional geographic structure was not the political barrier

In the east, the Confucian Philosophy became the anchor of peaceful governance which resulted from the lesson learned in the past civilizations. Likewise, the western sphere of influence demanded the same peaceful and righteous way to govern people way back the time of Plato and Socrates that even revived in the Age of Enlightenment. The blending of the east and west as part of the sphere of influence had been the same ideas of Change, Innovation, Idealism and Freedom even in the point of view of oriental and western philosophy.

This book expands the interpretation on the Final Continuum Phase Transformation of "Belt and Road Initiative" on the basis of the Maritime Silk Road for Asia, Africa and Europe :

1. **Political and Economic Philosophy of Change**. The primordial wisdom of the initiative dictates by the political change through the implementation of peaceful diplomatic activities of the sovereign state to participate the revival of the Maritime Silk Road that had been established for many centuries in China. This economic change provides the infrastructure and investment support to further improve the employment generation, reduce poverty, and other social benefits of the program.

2. **Political,   Economic and Technological Philosophy of Innovation.** This represents the continuum stage of economic development in the idea of change which is followed by innovation based on the scientific and technological development for trade and industry in the identified areas of the Maritime Silk Road in Asia, Africa and Europe. The economic programs of the "Belt and Road Initiative" emphasizes the technology transfer and establishment of trade and infrastructure networks to achieve economic development in the area.

3. **Social and Humane Philosophy in Idealism.** The third continuum level once achieve the political and economic change followed the technological innovation enhances the quality of life. This defines the social reality of class struggle will no longer the issue as the human society is given more economic opportunity to participate the "Belt and Road Initiative." The long term economic impact will provide the financial compensation and benefits within the ambit of employment generation, poverty alleviation and enterprise development.

4. **Achieving the Development Philosophy of Freedom** .This is the end of suffering because the long term economic effects in the implementation of the "Belt and Road Initiative" will give more opportunity of the human society to sustain the improvement of quality of life in a given society. This reduces the social exploitation and suffering to all beneficiaries of the program which economic development is the key criteria of fulfilling the development philosophy of freedom.

Key Concepts and Assumptions of the Philosophy of " Belt and Road Initiative" of the Maritime Silk Road

The key concepts and assumptions are operationally presented on the basis of the continuum level of philosophical development in the ideas of Change, Innovation, Idealism and Freedom. The author discusses the rational and constructive view of the "Belt and Road Initiative" as to the political and economic impact in dealing with peaceful diplomatic activities to ensure the successful implementation of the development programs to all the people in Asia, Africa and Europe.

Political Philosophy. It reflects the essence of noble intention and motive of a sovereign state to bring closer and peaceful relationships with mutual respect and recognition to provide social and economic services to improve the quality of life of the people. It also defines the government initiative in the implementation of the infrastructure investment and information technology support to deal with diplomatic ties with the Chinese Government through peaceful cooperation, bilateral and multi-lateral partnerships in response to the economic growth and development among countries of Asia, Africa and Europe.

1. **Employment Generation.** The infrastructure and investment supports provide the necessary employment and compensation including the direct effect in the economic materials input of the program.

2. **Poverty Alleviation.** The social and economic services given by the national government to provide employment and livelihood program to provide income and employment.

3. **Social and Economic Welfare.** The government responsibility to provide the necessary basic services such as Education, Health, Environment, Infrastructure support, agricultural services, livelihood program.

Economic Philosophy. The essence of the productive enterprise demands the useful financial support to any sovereign state that will spill-off in the increase of material resources and manufacturing outputs including the employment of citizens in the implementation of development programs under the " Belt and Road Initiative."

1. **Social Equity.** The economic support of the livelihood programs and employment of the underprivileged class that can be part of the recipients of the development program. It expected that the critical areas provided of support includes the agriculture, fishery, forestry, aqua-culture and other sectors that will benefits from the provisions of infrastructure and investment support.

2. **Economic Growth and Development.** The productive result of the development programs that will increase the Gross Domestic Product, Gross National Product, Infrastructure Investment and other financial benefits arrive at the program. The most important in this area is the economic development which contributed to the productive benefits of the poor people or the underprivileged class.

3. **Pro-Poor Economic Programs.** The utilization of technical assistance to give the necessary income and employment by providing livelihood enterprises, jobs and other forms of assistance.

Humane Philosophy. The equal social rights and opportunities of all people in a given society for the development of self-esteem, human dignity, freedom and live in descent life as a result of the financial grants and assistance in the infrastructure and business investment which will lead to higher employment opportunities and income derived of the poor people.

Self-Esteem. The direct economic benefits on the consciousness of the under privilege class (pro-poor program) to enjoy the financial compensation and provisions of materials goods including the equality of opportunity to all the stratified classes.

Human Dignity. The extended benefits for all the people of given society to enjoy the fruits of their labor to live in descent life

Freedom. The accumulation of material wealth and income will bring more economic opportunities for the poor people to enjoy the basic rights to own, use and dispose property. The freedom denotes the full conviction of decent life which adhered the rule of social equality to all mankind.

Decent Life. It is not simply the rights to live with social equality to all mankind but the full basic provisions of economic resources to let the family members enjoy in a decent shelter, education, health and other forms of basic needed to fully appreciate the meaning of quality life in a given society.

Idealism. The decent life attributed by economic change and innovation ensures the incorruptible action that cannot be socially exploited from the bondage of double standard view in the apex of social stratification.

Freedom. It denotes the end of continuum in the " Belt and Road Initiative" to bring peace and decent life as the *nirvana* of the social beneficiaries in the implementation of the Maritime Silk Road in Africa, Asia and Europe.

The continuum action in the assumption of the philosophical analysis of Change, Innovation, Idealism and Freedom will provide more in the mediated view of the political ideologies of the east-west. The main theme redounds in what we believe the equal rights for decent life that creates the nirvana of life. We should provide the bridge of hope and understanding by the sphere of influence by the east and west in creating concept of Idealism and Freedom including justice, equality and appreciating the idea of human rights . The political ideologies have the same path of social equality apprehension where synthesize actions have the presence of *dukkha (sufferings)* when power and authority in the rigid social structure destroys the very essence of human dignity.

The nirvana of the philosophical point of view of the " Belt and Road Initiative" is when peaceful cooperation and agreement on tangible infrastructure support for manufacturing and industrial sector, transportation, technology transfer, information technology and other mode of development assistance. The end economic results are innumerable particularly addressing a decent life that will work just like developed countries with bilateral and multi-lateral development programs. The social stratification will be expanded to presence of middle class that will have the collective consciousness in the appreciating the ideas of Change, Innovation, Idealism and Freedom.

The western hemisphere may agree that *nirvana* of humanity depends so much of giving decent life to all notwithstanding on race, culture, religion, ideology and beliefs. The humanity cannot attend the full ideals of freedom and dignity when decent life is not existed to them. There will always be social exploitation and suffering whether this is developed or industrialized counties, the sphere of influence of the east and west will always become the tirades of ideological conflicts from the perplexity of limited employment and income. The decent life has been there to all of us we never accepted the truth but we can promote them in the development action of Change, Innovation, Idealism and Freedom.

Chapter III
Human Essence and Philosophy of Change
in the Maritime Silk Road of the "Belt and Road Initiative"

When there is change the human adaptation has to provide the conformity of what is the new situation that appears in a given situation. This new situation arises human perplexity as how to adopt in its existence. It has to conform the modification of a new situation that appears in a given time. This will create human deviance and conflict arising such change which is known as dukkha (suffering). It is a prevailing condition when new situation will appear that created discomfort to all who will experience such change. The only way to reduce social deviance and conflict when this new situation is accepted wholeheartedly to work for common good.

The Maritime Silk Road emphasizes the economic change that has been practiced since the beginning of Chinese civilization. The infrastructure development was more on the Maritime Chinese ships that engaged in diplomacy trade across the continental routes of Asia as far as Africa. The Chinese diplomatic relations through economic trade had been well established in the kingdoms and tribes in the famous ports of Asia and Africa. The economic trade did not only prosper by the Chinese dynastic jars and other commodities but the main product of silk defined the new world order of economic activities.

The inherence of time element defines the moment of truth in the evolutionary nature of human society. It is the continuum existence that persist in the human activities revered by the common knowledge and attitude that must define the usual life process for the survival of mankind. Yet the beauty of time reveals element of change that adopted from the evolution of discovering something new from the earthly resources.

a)   *Change is a product of human activities based from discoveries and innovations of what can be developed in the material world.. This represents the by-product of scientific discoveries that had been tested throughout the evolutionary process of cognitive development for the purpose of improving specific life dimension. The dukkha (suffering) will reveal when this may not benefit the quality of life which had more used to the destruction of human life. Most the application of scientific discoveries are beneficial to human society that had been successfully produced good results in the economic growth and development. This can be further translated in the next phase of societal change which is known as innovation.*

The Maritime Silk Road responded the economic trade as part of the human activities that extended the vast continental waters in the Asia and Africa. The economic change had been well-established in the all frontiers of human endeavors that tested the real essence of diplomatic trade that came in with the many civilized states in Asia particularly Southeast Asia where the kingdoms and empires were distinctly connected based on the common regional cultures. In the history of the Maritime Silk Road not so much had been known as to the human tool of development for discoveries and innovations until the engagement period of the of colonial conquest of the western world. Actually, there had been peace and tranquility before the colonial conquest and imperialistic role of the west in Asia and Africa. The discoveries and inventions of China defined by the economic materials needed to a more comfortable life particularly the nobles (kings and chieftains) who opened their long diplomatic trade with the Chinese traders.

The Maritime Silk Road had been provided the transformation of quality of life in the discoveries and inventions of the varied used of economic products that prospered through the Chinese civilizations. The warring states were not so much affected by the maritime activities of the other established kingdoms and states throughout Asia and Africa. Furthermore, the discoveries and inventions of the military warfare subjugated the city-states were more on internal purpose that dictated the variants of the dynastic cycle of Chinese history. The Asian life was given more by the physiologic discoveries and inventions to improve the quality of life that transcended in the culture and heritage in a given kingdoms and states in the region. Finally, the economic transformation of products such as silk, spices, gold and jars became the lucrative maritime trade that even reached as far as Europe.

The economic product of silk became the famous fashion clothing of the Asian peoples particularly the nobles of the kingdoms and city-states of Southeast Asia. The spices derived from the east provided better food ingredients that became so exquisite to the luxurious dine of the royal and noble families. The jars and ceramics became the main instrument of economic diversification of reserving the food and home design in the classic history of the east. These have been the reasons why the west started to use the discoveries and inventions of modern warfare that changed the diplomatic limelight of the Asian dynastic cycle that later on the political image of economic change defined by the gradual emergence of ideas of Mercantilism, Colonialism and Imperialism. This represented the *dukkha* (sufferings) of all Asian and African peoples based from the economic beliefs that subjugation of kingdoms and states provided so much benefits to the western aggressors as the modern warfare were so much introduced by them that dynastic cycle became politically extinct from the Chinese civilization.

In contemporary time, the revival of the Maritime Silk Road defines the real essence of diplomatic economic activities particularly in the Southeast Asia which became the stronghold of high economic growth and development. The idea of economic change becomes so vibrant that the recent discoveries and inventions of the Information Technology wielded the high value of globalized commercialism. There are so much modification of improved IT programs that would embrace the continuous paradigm shift of economic products in the market. The *dukkha* has not embraced by the economic materialism of Information Technology as this will likely benefit by the technological change that rapidly happening in contemporary time. The nirvana of economic development denotes the new life cycle of the paradigm shift of the technological chips that have been modified to infuse the new world order where information and electronic technology represents the bulk of economic change in the 21st century.

b)   Change seems a by-product of human imaginations and actions that had been tested through experiments which then applied and utilized in the society.

The development process of change reveals the vicarious human activities to conduct experiments to prove a hypothetical assumptions. These are conducted as by-product of human imaginations and actions which are utilized for specific purpose which are either beneficial and destructive. The beneficial effects provide the necessary support of the improvement of human life that will further bring peace and development in a society. However, the dukkha (suffering) represents the possible destruction of human race as a result of greed and vanity. The human imaginations and actions when dukkha exists in this situation provides the interest and motive to exploit and suppress the society so that end goals are being achieved in expense of the enjoyment of life activities.

The Maritime Silk Road represents the beneficial effects in the economic growth and development in the Asian society. The Chinese civilization had been given much economic opportunity to expand the diplomatic relations with the Asian state. The beneficial side of the economic trade defined by the highly valuable Chinese products that utilized by the Asian states. The Chinese products had been there for centuries of dynastic development which served well its purpose particularly in the silk and jar products that spread throughout the Asian region.

The political upheavals of the Asian States were so intense that *dukkha* remained the pervasive force that corrupted by the diplomatic relationships. However, these were more on internal strife from the dynastic cycle of the rise and fall of kingdoms. The *dukka* was not the reflection and manifestation of the Maritime Silk Road because the economic diplomacy enforced the political obligation of the State. The economic vibrancy became so revealing through the rise of civilized states in the Asian region.

c) *Change is the continuum element of time that justifies productive endeavor of human society.*

The historical perspectives of change explored the achievement and productivity to transform for a more complex society. This represents the ideal state of human society wherein the discoveries and inventions are transformed to beneficial in their physiologic needs. It had been revered form of societal development. that this was part of the economic materialism. The continuum element of time reflects the historicity of the gradual development of functional trade and industry, transportation, buildings that reconstitute the platform of economic growth and development. However, the pervasive issue remained to put the emphasis of dukkha was the political upheavals that degenerated the moral and ethical life in the civilized society.

The Maritime Silk Road ensured the continuum effort of the economic diplomacy for centuries of Asian contacts. The continuum element of change revealed by the improvement and development of human society. The continuum elements of time had been well-managed that synthesized the contemporary life.

The presence of the Maritime Silk Road was reflected by the economic activities with varied Chinese products distributed through the Asian continents. In the Chinese civilization, it dictated so much on economic diplomacy through trade and commerce by providing the silk, jar and porcelains. The continuum of commerce and industry had been well defined and managed by the Asian countries for many centuries as part of the economic interdependence of sovereign states. It became the lucrative business which attracted by the royal and noble families particularly the Chinese products that could be used in the interior design and kitchenware's that symbolized class stratification in the notable Asian kingdoms.

These vibrant commerce and industries were not severely damaged by the continuum of international diplomacy that even the rise and fall of Asian kingdoms did not affect such political change. However, the western domination in Asia broke the economic and political continuum that affected kingdoms and states which could no longer control a sovereign government that had been existed in centuries of economic interdependence dictated by the amity and comity of the Chinese government. Even the Chinese dynastic cycle became extinct in its political stability for many centuries and the western domination totally changed the continuum economic stability of the maritime silk road.

The *dukkha* of the political and economic continuum existed by the western domination ended the peaceful interdependence of the kingdoms and dynasties in Asia. It was no longer the same when the amalgamation and assimilation process went through the Asian cultural line that the international trade as originally existed by the maritime silk road changed forever.

In contemporary time, the economic resurgence of the Maritime Silk Road provides the revival of the authentic diplomatic existence based on independent foreign policy that can be traced back by the friendly relations of kingdoms and dynasties in Asia. The revival of Asian economic activities based on the Maritime Silk Road empowered the peoples' of Asia as one continent from its theme of "Belt and Road Initiative." The Chinese government has been pushing this theme because of its moral sovereign relation with all nations of Asia.

d) *Change is the culmination of human activities that designed to improve the quality of life can be applied in economic development.*

The existence of human society evolves from the metamorphosis of mind in search of food, shelter and clothing as the basic ingredients of life structures and processes. For thousands of years, the Paleolithic and Neolithic Age exemplified the gradual revolving of human activities in search of food and shelter with little emphasis in clothing. These had been the limelight of human survivals which was *dukkha* (sufferings) in the its societal existence.

In the study of change, it is the by-product of human imaginations and actions that had been experienced in the search of better physiologic life which then transformed what is known as economic materialism. The basic needs defined the existence of life from simple way to get food through hunting and fishing, provision of clothing and shelter, and to learn to live with language and adopt the environment that defined societal culture. These way of life existed hundreds of years that later on generically transformed the human society by the gradual multi-dimensional characteristics in the economic, social, political, spiritual and moral, technological development.

These multi-dimensional characteristics defined the human society that generically presented in the civilization of the past. The civilization of the past provided the grandeur of the existence of human society that pervaded to the beginning of *dukkha* (suffering). The exquisite civilization had been the mentor of sufferings that exploited the human society where change was existed as a result of social stratification where nobles, military leaders, and royal families enjoyed the luxury of life where the peasants suffered so much from the societal situations of conquest and class exploitation. The grandeur of the civilization of the past provided the dukkha (suffering) that must be existed in conformity of the moral and spiritual development of mankind.

In the idea of innovation, it represents the learning and absorbing new cultures that created and transferred from the introduction of new inventions and discoveries in a given society. However, the perplexity of change defines the societal deviation that may not be acceptable or there is an altered condition that may affect the culture which may be beneficial in the development of mankind.

What is important in the end-product of innovation defines the twinning accommodation of idealism and freedom. Once societal change has beneficial effect to mankind cascaded in the development of innovation that will absorb a new set of cultures. This will be the basis of substantial change where the idealistic principles of mankind which provides good faith and creative thinking. This is the true essence of life when the mind is liberated from what is achieved in change, innovation and idealism which is now known as freedom.

The idea of freedom liberates oneself with wisdom, it suggests the path leading the end of the suffering (magga). The essence of freedom does not simply mean a democratic principles of the western world where there is the existence of political exploitation and sufferings of the masses. The rich becomes richer the poor becomes poorer because the democratic ideas are bounded by human interests on profit and motive. This is not the true essence of freedom because the poor people suffered so much for the sake of achieving democracy. The essence of freedom defines the quality of life among the peoples of the world to live in equality, justice and compassion to human society.

This can only be achieved when economic materialism has given support to all in the paradigm shift of world peace and development that change, innovation, idealism and freedom defined by the historical roots of the civilization of Asia. The continuum of development process on the true essence of freedom had already well established in the historical activities of the Maritime Silk Road in the Asian region that now evolved in the contemporary analysis of "Belt and Road Initiative."

Chapter IV
'Belt and Road Initiative" in the
Political and Economic Philosophy of Change

The changing perspective of the world order has been connected by the perplexing mindset of the societal role to embrace the literal translations of human activities that molded the disparity and conflict of a universal ideology in embracing the traditional beliefs and perceptions of human thought. The advocacy of world peace and development has reflected not only in the spiritual, moral or ideological beliefs but the human understanding of the basic facts on the genuine meaning of change, innovation, idealism and freedom in the mindset of culture and knowledge. The rational meanings of these terms have promoted the divergence of time element and the embodiment of the universal understanding from our human perceptions to embrace the positive aura of cultural life.

The historical evolution of the Maritime Silk Road defines the borderless action of human trade and culture from highly diversified and distinctive taste of political scenario that existed on calm and friendly relations of state order. The oneness of society of the maritime silk road defines what are now in the present but no one can unify the interdependence of the sovereign society particularly in the Asian region. The spiritual and cultural values provided the reflection of the true meaning of human actions working together to the political and economic progress of the nation. There was no disparity of rules in the freedom of navigation of the maritime silk road which already defined the Asian people living in peace and harmony of the sovereign states.

More than two millennia ago the diligent and courageous people of Eurasia explored and opened up several routes of trade and cultural exchanges that linked the major civilizations of Asia, Europe and Africa, collectively called the Silk Road by later generations. For thousands of years, the Silk Road Spirit – "peace and cooperation, openness and inclusiveness, mutual learning and mutual benefit" – has been passed from generation to generation, promoted the progress of human civilization, and contributed greatly to the prosperity and development of the countries along the Silk Road. Symbolizing communication and cooperation between the East and the West, the Silk Road Spirit is a historic and cultural heritage shared by all countries around the world. (Vision and Action of the Maritime Silk Road)

The economic historicity of the contemporary maritime silk road situation provides the clear path of reducing the perennial existence of *dukkha* in the western domination of political and economic ideas of deception. The bipolar interpretation can be dictated by the very existence of political and economic extinction of the maritime silk road in western world domination. The fear of the western world by the Chinese government action may repeat the perplexity of the political agenda when the maritime silk road was destroyed by the essence of world domination.

The lifelong learnings revolved by the demand of increasing knowledge within the periphery of the sovereign states of Asia where the oldest civilization ensured the universal value of respect and recognition of the neighboring states. This is based on the forefront of the historical discoveries and innovations that embraced the Asian people as the necessity to use for the improvement of human activities. In the history of our time, the maritime silk road provided the economic and political support to embrace development variations that made the Asian people became closer together that brought peace and security where the diplomacy worked particularly in the center of sovereign Asian power. Yet the political and economic knowledge of the closeness and oneness of the Asian people undermined by the bipolar interpretation of facts and the changing sovereign closeness to the other parts of the world.

The political and economic reconciliation of the maritime silk road has to be justified from the historicity of the Asian states where "oneness and closeness" became the authentic societal facts. This is the unilateral interpretation of sovereign closeness that western countries cannot questioned. There were no political or economic dominations existed by the diplomatic interdependence attached in the contemporary maritime silk road. Whether the bipolar interpretation is real or not for the existence of the contemporary maritime silk road as initiated by the Chinese government may not harm the sovereign state of Asia. The Chinese foreign investments of tangible infrastructure as part of commitment to implement the maritime silk road network in Asia will ensure economic growth and development.

The divisiveness of the Asian society never been corrupted by the original civilization of time when economic and political prosperity brought the peace of the land. There were equal sovereign Asian states that peripheral old civilization of the east defined the spirit of oneness and closeness. This was brought about by the development of maritime silk road where economic and political prosperity achieved the peaceful evolution of time. The idea of change had been politically and economically correct in the human activities of the maritime silk road that defined the interchange of the products even at the time of the reconnected trade for spices. However, the essence of change became perplexing when political apprehension of those with interest from the culturally distinct society who never understood the Asian people. In the perplexing knowledge of the infinite of the world civilization, the societal change provided the boundaries and distinctive meaning that could no longer refined in the contemporary time.

The dichotomy of knowledge had been viewed by the polarity of ideas in the east and west for the meaning of change. The civilizations of the Asian people have been revolving the essence of what is now the democratic and civilized society. In the Asian region, the idea of world peace has already been there for us to embrace the genuine meaning of freedom. The maritime silk road defined that world order that unconsciously defining the meaning of change from the continuum model of technological development during the apex of Asian civilization. There had been innovation in the past that catapulted the dynamic civilization into its peak of economic and political development. What had been adopted in the past civilization was focused on the technological change where idealism was represented by the understanding of the mutual respect and recognition among the Asian people and extended to the people of the west. The idea of freedom may mean different perspective in the Asian context when the sustainable economic trade and diplomacy that defined by hundreds of years where mutual respect and amity appeared from one another. Therefore, the essence of freedom ensures the recognition and appreciation of economic rights that will prevent any forms of suppression and exploitation of the masses.

What lessons of economic and political philosophy represent the maritime silk road that had been well established in the Asian states that attained freedom, peace and amity among the sovereign nations? This question represents the metamorphosis of time in the development activities of the Maritime Silk Road in Asia. Hence, the essence of this activity represents the continuum process of analyzing the synergy of the contemporary application of the Confucius Institute of Maritime Silk Road which has defined the meaning of world peace through change, innovation, idealism and freedom.

These are the cyclical world peace mechanisms that presented the harmony of human society from its traditional view on the political and economic philosophy of the contemporary time. Furthermore, it is a paradigm shift of world peace in understanding the human society which embraces the continuum mechanisms of world peace to prevent from the increasing polarity of knowledge that later on defined by the debacle of political and economic struggles. The world exists from the common ground of understanding in the sovereign states on the societal beliefs and actions in the existence of mankind for the quality of life for all. There is no polarity of dichotomy that ensembles in this principle of quality of life where sovereign states exist to provide the social services through general and common welfare to all. The existence of United Nations focuses on this view from the world peace concepts in the delivery of government services defined by inclusive growth and development, employment generation, security and safety, sustainable development, science and technology development, cultural diversity and other relevant undertakings to achieve the concept of the quality of life.

Paradigm Shift of World Peace through "Belt and Road Initiative"

The clarity of peaceful coexistence redounds in the "Belt and Road Initiative" is in line with the purposes and principles of the UN Charter. It upholds the Five (5) Principles of Peaceful Coexistence: mutual respect for each other's sovereignty and territorial integrity, mutual non-aggression, mutual non-interference in each other's internal affairs, equality and mutual benefit, and peaceful coexistence.

The concept of change revolves the transformation, conversion and modification of future practice or action that usually create instability and difference from the usual things that we doing in the society. In the paradigm shift of change, the idea does not mean radicalism or abrupt transformation nor systemic shifting of interest from the understanding of amity or comity among nations. The change refers the positive dimension of life that brings continual world peace that would embrace and support the wide range of societal development for all nations.

The perspective of change the political, economic and cultural stability has brought about the articulation of innovative life through discoveries and inventions that had been there throughout the centuries of human existence. As in the case of the Maritime Silk Road, the political life had improved the relations of the Asian states because of the constant trade visits blending to understand the product development. These were the technological discoveries and innovations that improved the quality of life of the human society in Asia. The development effects affected by the western world that attracted the diffusion of knowledge until the change of mindset in the industrial revolution that fade the way to create a new order of egocentric technological development that defined the present generation.

The Maritime Silk Road had the good model of political life which the sovereign nations respected the ideas of wholesome development of the state where independence and freedom existed vis-à-vis to technological innovations. The sovereign states transformed into dynamic and vibrant economic order with good diplomatic ties among nations of the Asian. In contemporary time, this has been achieved by the industrialized states of Asia. The political and economic philosophy may be different from the western nations but the genuine principles are still reflective in its underlying principles of quality of life. The idea of world peace must always bring the principles of amity and comity which the sovereign states are doing now. Yet, world peace must be closer that what must be expected by the standard ideas of amity and comity in recognition of sovereign existence. The mutual trust and interest to achieve quality of life among the nations of the world must be achieved through political engagements on the idea of world peace not on systems of the government. The touching and embracing mutual respect must be within the essence of human reciprocity to closely touch the political diversity and empathy with diplomatic humility rather than antagonism.

The essence of political humility and meekness may not define the strength of sovereign nations but can work well with empathy and understanding that even a highly diversified political system may bring closer their heart and soul in the engagement of improving the quality of life for all. This may be done in the technological engagement for closer relationships among nations of the world. The radical change of our society now is reflective in the technical operations among the sovereign nations that had been present the historical roots of the Maritime Silk Road where the borderless trade society had been working well to all Asian nations.

The idea of freedom had been existed in the past yet the political blending of the contemporary time must be reflective from the political understanding and empathy. The economic trade had defined the kind of technological change that innovation becomes the next cycle of development to improve the quality of life for all. Yet political scientists remained adamant as to the issue of freedom as distinct in the study of political system where the rule of authoritarianism is deeply embedded in such ideology. In the case of the Maritime Silk Road of past, the authoritarian rule had existed in the political belief to control and regulate the government resources with wide latitude of freedom and innovation. This has been happening in Asia which represents the natural flow of political rule that suppression of freedom has not been in the forefront of technological innovation and idealism to achieve the quality of life as always envisioned by Asian nations.

The history of Asian nations has been concentrated by the dynamic and flexible political system embodied by cultural understanding on freedom and technological innovation. The political development during the Maritime Silk Road period had been known to the Asian nations where democratic ideas were contemplated by the essence of human freedom through the navigation of cultural and economic diffusion. The Asian nations instilled the ideas of patriotism, sacrifice, self-discipline and commitment where engraved by responsible human freedom for all. The human freedom ensures the inclusivity of economic growth and development where equality of society embraces this idea not a disparity of social class. The idea of social equality embraces the conception of human modality that government defines the best interest of the Asian people. This presents the highest degree of freedom to attain world peace not a superficial democratic ideals with an outcome of suppression, exploitation, racial and social discrimination .

World Peace and Development Mechanisms for "Belt and Road Initiative" of Chinese President Xi Jinping

In contemporary time, the "Belt and Road Initiative" of Chinese President XI Jinping provides the remarkable transformations of the political, cultural and economic diplomacy among the sovereign nations of Asia, Africa and Europe. In the "Belt and Road Initiative," it describes the development continuum based on the prescribed economic philosophy of social and technological change to attain quality of life among the participating countries in the world.

The idea of **Change in Belt and Road Initiative** of the Chinese President Xi Jinping represents the revival of the Maritime Silk Road that defines the modification and transformation of the modern economic activities through the partnership and linkages in the Asian region. This provides the support of social , economic and technological change from the emerging market of Asia through the leadership and support of the Chinese government bringing the former glory of the civilization in the Far East. Notably, the Chinese civilization had established diplomatic ties that existed in the maritime silk road which spread throughout the kingdoms and empires of Asia, Europe and Africa.

It infuses the development and improvement of human society that enhances the quality of life as a result of capital and labor intensive industry. Regardless of political and economic system, the idea of transformation defined by freedom of enterprise and navigation to engage with the Asian resources which benefits the human society for the improvement of the quality of life. The engagement of change redounds to the technical assistance of technology transfer, infrastructure support and infusion of fresh capital to the Asian region. It is not a radical social development but the freedom of human enterprise to discover and innovate to improve the production of goods in the international market.

The technological change defines a borderless society controlled by responsible corporate ownership to innovate the products for the freedom of enterprise that will exist in the market. The political dynamics of change disposes economic freedom through innovation that will deal in the global market. The "One Belt One Road" rejuvenates the genuine direction of change in the existence of freedom of enterprise. Furthermore, the political engagement of sovereign nations denotes the obvious direction of diplomatic peace for mutual understanding a respect and recognition of power structure. The trust and confidence building is directed with equal share of resources and investments which can be done through bilateral and multilateral negotiations to expand the economic growth and development of the area.

Chapter V
'Belt and Road Initiative" in the
Political, Economic and Technological Philosophy of Innovation

It reflects the continuum model of change by adopting " One Belt One Road" to identify and determine the strategic opportunity for technological support needed for the diplomatic engagement which is productive to inclusive growth and development. The development of industrialized countries defines this method of change through capital-intensive enterprise. The "Belt and Road Initiative" provides the support of technological innovation for investment and infrastructure support.

There are economic engagement for those countries participating in the "One Belt One Road" in the utilization of trained manpower including educated scientists and engineers to conduct Research and Development Program to ensure the sustained technological development in different field of expertise. This will give authentic and innovative scientific researches in providing technical cooperation to implement "One Belt One Road. The inclusiveness of the technological development imposes the much needed break of the poor sector of society for their participation in the R and D program.

The "Belt and Road Initiative" has the political, economic and technological philosophy of Innovation that can be justified by the idea of the Chinese government through the regional cooperation priorities based on the Vision and Actions on Jointly Silk Road Economic Belt and 21st Century Maritime Silk Road provides the mutual complementation in the regional cooperation which should promote policy coordination, facilities connectivity, unimpeded trade, financial integration and people-to-people bonds as their five major goals, and strengthen cooperation in the following key areas: (1) Policy Coordination ; (2) Facilities Connectivity; (3) Unimpeded trade; (4) Financial Integration; and (5) People to People bond."

1) **Policy Coordination.** This provides the intergovernmental cooperation by building a macro policy exchange and communication mechanism, expand shared interests, enhance mutual political trust, and reach new cooperation consensus. In support of the "Belt and Road Initiative." The participating countries may fully coordinate their economic development strategies and policies, work out plans and measures for regional cooperation, negotiate to solve cooperation-related issues, and jointly provide policy support for the implementation of practical cooperation and large-scale projects.

The political philosophy transcends in the diplomatic trust to provide the regional development support of the idea of "oneness and openness" of the sovereign state to initiate the best interest of the society on innovative opportunities to work together in the general and common welfare for all.

2) **Facilities Connectivity.** The priority areas in this initiative are the improvement of the connectivity of their infrastructure construction plans and technical standard systems, jointly push forward the construction of international trunk passageways, and form an infrastructure network connecting all sub-regions in Asia, and between Asia, Europe and Africa step by step.

   2.1 Promotion of green and low-carbon infrastructure construction and operation management, taking into full account the impact of climate change on the construction.

   2.2 Construction of transport infrastructure for key passageways, junctions and projects, and give priority to linking up unconnected road sections, removing transport bottlenecks, advancing road safety facilities and traffic management facilities and equipment, and improving road network connectivity.

   2.3 Building a unified coordination mechanism for whole-course transportation, increase connectivity of customs clearance, reloading and multimodal transport between countries, and gradually formulate compatible and standard transport rules, so as to realize international transport facilitation.

   2.4 Construction of port infrastructure to build smooth land water transportation channels, and advance port cooperation; increase sea routes and the number of voyages, and enhance information technology cooperation in maritime logistics.

   2.5 Expansion and building the platforms and mechanisms for comprehensive civil aviation cooperation, and quicken our pace in improving aviation infrastructure.

   2.6 Promotion of cooperation in the connectivity of energy infrastructure, work in concert to ensure the security of oil and gas pipelines and other transport routes, build cross-border power supply networks and power-transmission routes, and cooperate in regional power grid upgrading and transformation.

2.7 Promotion of joint ventures in the advancement of the construction of cross-border optical cables and other communications trunk line networks, improve international communications connectivity, and create an Information Silk Road.

2.8 Building the bilateral cross-border optical cable networks at a quicker pace, plan transcontinental submarine optical cable projects, and improve spatial (satellite) information passageways to expand information exchanges and cooperation.

3. **Unimpeded Trade.** The investment and trade cooperation includes the improve investment and trade facilitation, and remove investment and trade barriers for the creation of a sound business environment within the region and in all related countries. This is done through the opening of free trade areas so as to unleash the potential for expanded cooperation. The participating countries provide the support to enhance customs cooperation such as information exchange, mutual recognition of regulations, and mutual assistance in law enforcement; improve bilateral and multilateral cooperation in the fields of inspection and quarantine, certification and accreditation, standard measurement, and statistical information; and work to ensure that the WTO Trade Facilitation Agreement takes effect and is implemented.

3.1 Improvement the customs clearance facilities of border ports, establish a "single-window" in border ports, reduce customs clearance costs, and improve customs clearance capability. Furthermore, the increase of cooperation in supply chain safety and convenience, improve the coordination of cross-border supervision procedures, promote online checking of inspection and quarantine certificates, and facilitate mutual recognition of Authorized Economic Operators. It also includes the lowering of non-tariff barriers, jointly improving the transparency of technical trade measures, and enhancing trade liberalization and facilitation.

3.2 Expansion of trading areas, including the improvement of trade structure, exploration of new growth areas of trade, and promotion of trade balance. Furthermore, making innovations in our forms of trade, and development cross-border e-commerce and other modern business models. A service trade support system is set up to consolidate and expand conventional trade, and efforts to develop modern service trade should be strengthened. This also includes the integration of investment and trade, and promotion trade through investment.

3.3 Enhancement of investment facilitation including the elimination of investment barriers, and push forward negotiations on bilateral investment protection agreements and double taxation avoidance agreements to protect the lawful rights and interests of investors.

3.4 Expansion of mutual investment areas, deepen cooperation in agriculture, forestry, animal husbandry and fisheries, agricultural machinery manufacturing and farm produce processing, and promote cooperation in marine-product farming, deep-sea fishing, aquatic product processing, seawater desalination, marine biopharmacy, ocean engineering technology, environmental protection industries, marine tourism and other fields.

3.5 Cooperation in the exploration and development of coal, oil, gas, metal minerals and other conventional energy sources; advance cooperation in hydropower, nuclear power, wind power, solar power and other clean, renewable energy sources; and promote cooperation in the processing and conversion of energy and resources at or near places where they are exploited, so as to create an integrated industrial chain of energy and resource cooperation including enhance cooperation in deep processing technology, equipment and engineering services in the fields of energy and resources.

3.6 Promotion of the emerging industries through the new-generation information technology, biotechnology, new energy technology, new materials and other emerging industries, and establish entrepreneurial and investment cooperation mechanisms.

3.7 Improvement of the division of labor and distribution of industrial chains by encouraging the entire industrial chain and related industries to develop in concert; establish R&D, production and marketing systems; and improve industrial supporting capacity and the overall competitiveness of regional industries. Addition to this, it provides the openness of the service industry to each other to accelerate the development of regional service industries.

3.8 Exploration of a new mode of investment cooperation, working together to build all forms of industrial parks such as overseas economic and trade cooperation zones and cross-border economic cooperation zones, and promote industrial cluster development.

3.9 Promotion of the ecological progress in conducting investment and trade, increase cooperation in conserving eco-environment, protecting biodiversity, and tackling climate change, and join hands to make the Silk Road an environment-friendly one.

The "Belt and Road Initiative" welcomes the companies from all countries to invest in Asian countries through the leadership of Chinese government, and encourage Chinese enterprises to participate in infrastructure construction in other countries along the Belt and Road, and make industrial investments there. There is also a support localized operations and management of Chinese companies to boost the local economy, increase local employment, improve local livelihood, and take social responsibilities in protecting local biodiversity and eco-environment.

4. Financial Integration. This provides the support on financial cooperation, and makes more efforts in building a currency stability system, investment and financing system and credit information system in Asia.

4.1 Expansion of the scope and scale of bilateral currency swap and settlement with other countries along the Belt and Road, open and develop the bond market in Asia, make joint efforts to establish the Asian Infrastructure Investment Bank and BRICS New Development Bank, conduct negotiation among related parties on establishing Shanghai Cooperation Organization (SCO) financing institution, and set up and put into operations the Silk Road Fund as early as possible.

4.2 Strengthen practical cooperation of China ASEAN Interbank Association and SCO Interbank Association, and carry out multilateral financial cooperation in the form of syndicated loans and bank credit. This Chinese government will support the efforts of governments of the countries along the Belt and Road and their companies and financial institutions with good credit-rating to issue Renminbi bonds in China. Qualified Chinese financial institutions and companies are encouraged to issue bonds in both Renminbi and foreign currencies outside China, and use the funds thus collected in countries along the Belt and Road.

4.3 Strengthen financial regulation cooperation, encourage the signing of MOUs on cooperation in bilateral financial regulation, and establish an efficient regulation coordination mechanism in the region.

4.4 Improvement of the system of risk response and crisis management, build a regional financial risk early-warning system, and create an exchange and cooperation mechanism of addressing cross-border risks and crisis. This can be done through the increase cross-border exchange and cooperation between credit investigation regulators, credit investigation institutions and credit rating institutions. The Chinese government will also give full play to the role of the Silk Road Fund and that of sovereign wealth funds of countries along the Belt and Road, and encourage commercial equity investment funds and private funds to participate in the construction of key projects of the Initiative.

5. **People-to-people bond** . This is done by the spirit of friendly cooperation of the Silk Road by promoting extensive cultural and academic exchanges, personnel exchanges and cooperation, media cooperation, youth and women exchanges and volunteer services, so as to win public support for deepening bilateral and multilateral cooperation.

5.1 Promotion of the Students Exchange Programs by providing scholarships to the countries along the Belt and Road every year. This can be done by holding culture years, arts festivals, film festivals, TV weeks and book fairs in each other's countries; cooperate on the production and translation of fine films, radio and TV programs.

In the World Cultural Heritage sites, we should also increase personnel exchange and cooperation between countries along the Belt and Road. We should enhance cooperation in and expand the scale of tourism; hold tourism promotion weeks and publicity months in each other's countries; jointly create competitive international tourist routes and products with Silk Road features; and make it more convenient to apply for tourist visa in countries along the Belt and Road. We should push forward cooperation on the 21st-Century Maritime Silk Road cruise tourism program. We should carry out sports exchanges and support countries along Belt and Road in their bid for hosting major international sports events.

We should strengthen cooperation with neighboring countries on epidemic information sharing, the exchange of prevention and treatment technologies and the training of medical professionals, and improve our capability to jointly address public health emergencies. We will provide medical assistance and emergency medical aid to relevant countries, and carry out practical cooperation in maternal and child health, disability rehabilitation, and major infectious diseases including AIDS, tuberculosis and malaria. We will also expand cooperation on traditional medicine.

We should increase our cooperation in science and technology, establish joint labs (or research centers), international technology transfer centers and maritime cooperation centers, promote sci-tech personnel exchanges, cooperate in tackling key sci-tech problems, and work together to improve sci-tech innovation capability.

We should integrate existing resources to expand and advance practical cooperation between countries along the Belt and Road on youth employment, entrepreneurship training, vocational skills development, social security management, public administration and management and in other areas of common interest.

We should give full play to the bridging role of communication between political parties and parliaments, and promote friendly exchanges between legislative bodies, major political parties and political organizations of countries along the Belt and Road. We should carry out exchanges and cooperation among cities, encourage major cities in these countries to become sister cities, focus on promoting practical cooperation, particularly cultural and people-to-people exchanges, and create more lively examples of cooperation. We welcome the think tanks in the countries along the Belt and Road to jointly conduct research and hold forums.

We should increase exchanges and cooperation between nongovernmental organizations of countries along the Belt and Road, organize public interest activities concerning education, health care, poverty reduction, biodiversity and ecological protection for the benefit of the general public, and improve the production and living conditions of poverty-stricken areas along the Belt and Road. We should enhance international exchanges and cooperation on culture and media, and leverage the positive role of the Internet and new media tools to foster harmonious and friendly cultural environment and public opinion.

These are the common cooperation priorities for the academic community (for Universities and Colleges) in support of the educational, cultural and social processes for the Vision and Actions on Jointly Silk Road Economic Belt and 21st Century Maritime Silk Road :

1. Promote the extensive cultural and academic exchanges, personnel exchanges, and cooperation, media cooperation, youth and women exchanges and volunteer services, so as to win public support for deepening bilateral and multilateral cooperation.

2. *Promote* tourism activities relevant to the routes and products with Maritime Silk Road.

3. Strengthen the training of medical professionals, epidemic information sharing, the exchange of prevention and treatment technologies

4. Improve the capability to jointly address public health emergencies by providing medical assistance and emergency medical aid to relevant countries, and carry out practical cooperation in maternal and child health, disability rehabilitation, and major infectious diseases including AIDS, tuberculosis and malaria including the expansion of cooperation on traditional medicine.

5. Promote science and technology by establishing joint labs (or research centers), international technology transfer centers and maritime cooperation centers, promote sci-tech personnel exchanges, including cooperation in tackling key sci-tech problems, and work together to improve sci-tech innovation capability.

6. Integrate existing resources to expand and advance practical cooperation between countries along the Belt and Road on youth employment, entrepreneurship training, vocational skill development, social security management, public administration and management and in other areas of common interest

Chapter VI
'Belt and Road Initiative" in the Social and Humane Philosophy in Idealism and in Achieving the Development Philosophy of Freedom

The requisites of idealism reflect from the ladder of development in change and innovation. The economic change defines the revival of the maritime silk road as the strategic opportunity to bring further infrastructure and information technology investments in Asia and Africa. The continental and regional priorities are determined by the less developed countries or the third world that need more investments to address current concern of poverty and exploitation.

It is the metamorphosis of the continuum of change and innovation which is reflective from the achieve results of the technological development in the implementation of "Belt and Road Initiative." Likewise, it is the reflection of the quality of life in the achievement of change and innovation. The life satisfaction with the presence of comforts as a result of gainful employment and high income reduces the level of social deviance as manifested by superficial democratic ideals through exploitation and discrimination. The main ingredients of idealism ensure self-esteem, respect and freedom. These are the main reasons on the existence of the government to envision and to achieve employment generation with high income and resources addressing inclusive growth, awareness of sustainable development, good economic investment and infrastructure development of all sectors of the society.

This will further transform inner character of peace with self-esteem, dignity and freedom are well preserved by the stand point of ideal attitude with high level of professionalism. The perplexity of corruptible mind is fully prevented in the adherence of change and innovation. The less corruptible society has precedence of change and innovation which has been achieved in Europe and America. The less developed countries are more exposed to corruption because of social burden of poverty, hunger, dependency and exploitation. The democratic ideals will not solve the social problems of the poor masses that hunger and poverty drives them to become corrupt and victims of exploitation.

The idealistic value of human society has to consider the economic growth and development to support the basic needs in the transformation of the common welfare through the national goal of improved quality of life. The human perplexity imposes the social problems in the reality of societal existence of urban poor, squatter areas, rampant prostitution, criminality and injustice, malnutrition ,and other means of human exploitation and suffering of the deprived subjects in the sovereign state. The promotion of idealism emphasizes the human condition of the inequality of social class determined by the economic value of income and employment. This has been social deprivation of the material world that the monetary value as provided in income , saving and employment will defines the quality of life existed in the society. It is not the political ideology that responds the political and economic value of life but the presence of descent living where lies the true meaning of idealism.

The "Belt and Road Initiative" is not the perplexity of political agenda that defines the inner development goal as implemented through infrastructure and information technology investments but the social reality of economic value to improve the quality of life particularly in Africa and Asia. The idealistic point of view on humane life gradually defines what is later on transform the magnitude of economic and political change that will respond the nirvana of life from the perspective of idealism to its transform of the final step to achieve the full meaning of freedom. It is expected that its social transformation ensures the gradual perfection of human society as to the economic benefits of a country once joined the revival of the maritime silk road for Asia and Africa.

Social and Humane Philosophy of Idealism through the Maritime Silk Road Confucius Institute

The conceptualization of the Social and Humane Philosophy of Idealism denotes the long term economic and social benefits through the implementation of the " Belt and Road Initiative." The social development goals along poverty alleviation, economic development, employment generation that will balance the equality of society.

These are the salient features of the Social and Humane Philosophy of Idealism that will implement the priority areas of the "Belt and Road Initiative" through the road map of the Maritime Silk Road :

1. The political and economic change represents the core development transition to a humane life.

2. The economic and technological innovation defines the humane transition by the infrastructure and information technology as invested by the Chinese government in the "Belt and Road Initiative."

3. The manifested humane transition will be the recipients of the economic and information technology assistance that can be

translated in employment and national added value of the national investment of the " Belt and Road Initiative."

4. The social transition of the underprivileged class to be benefited by the employment and investment support in the identified area of economic development in the "Belt and Road Initiative."

5. The actual economic benefits ensure the real meaning of idealism through the employment and investments that will create high level of income and employment.

Therefore the conceptualization of idealism represents the full cycle of economic development in the "Belt and Road Initiative" that can transform to the social development of high level of self-esteem, dignity of life, equality of rights and privileges, and improved quality of life in the human society.

A. Continuum of the Social and Humane Philosophy in Reaching the Idealism

The political change does not rely on the government ideology but the concern on the necessary support of the general welfare program along the basic services. It requires the governmental support on employment, education, health and other basic provisions in order to sustain decent life of all the subjects of a sovereign state. The political idealistic view depends so much of how civilized sovereign state to contribute the best interest of the subjects to deal with the basic life support for employment and income as a means to serve the interest for common welfare.

In the case of economic change, the sustained production of goods and services that relied so much on international trade and manufacturing embodied the real essence of economic growth and development. The economic growth determines the capacity of sovereign state to sustain the Gross National Product (GNP) and Gross Domestic Product (GDP) with the support of the manufacturing sector and the presence of international trade. The economic change on the Chinese government's thrust of the "Belt and Road Initiative" in the Maritime Silk Road encourages the affected sovereign states in Asia and Africa to join the crusades in the economic growth and development. The Chinese investments are part of the economic change perceived in the "Belt and Road Initiative" to bring closer in the ideas of "Oneness and Closeness" particularly in the Asian region. Primarily, the Chinese government support on infrastructure and information connectivity demands more employment and investments that can increase the economic capacity to live for better life of the human society.

In the case of the economic innovation, it has been the latest development in the field of business and industry that can spill off through the technology transfer coming from the support of the Chinese government to complement the implementation of "Belt and Road initiative." The international partnerships of Chinese corporations bring more technological innovation to produce the local products that can compete in the global market. The "Belt and Road Initiative" established by the Chinese government introduces the new mechanism of international trade from the identified partner in the Maritime Silk Road to revive the diplomatic ties that had been working well for many centuries particularly in Asia.

In contemporary, the "Belt and Road Initiative" brings the Chinese investments on infrastructure support such as transport system and manufacturing sector that can be utilized as an effective instrument to provide income and employment to the Less Developed Countries (LDCs) or even to those with closed diplomatic ties to continue its existence in the development of the Maritime Silk Road. The idea of humane transition reflects on the lack of employment and limited income because the sovereign state has no enough infrastructure investments to continue the economic activities. However, the "Belt and Road Initiative" does not only give infrastructure support to the less developed countries but also to the developed countries in Asia where the main instrument of political stability and respect of sovereign state on independent foreign policy to commit for peaceful diplomatic ties to achieve the universal goal of " Oneness and Closeness" by initiating the same political path for many centuries the maritime silk road in Africa and Asia. It is always the best interest of the sovereign state even the economy is fully developed to commit and work together the interdependence of sovereign state.

Therefore, essence of idealism in the economic and technological innovation is the presence of international commitment to achieve the universal rights of the human society to be given enough employment, income and education that can be addressed in the "Belt and Road Initiative" for Asia and Africa. The idealistic economic structure demands the diplomatic support of multi-lateral agreement for the international community to work together in achieving the universal goal of " Belt and Road Initiative."

In the Vision and Actions on Jointly Building Silk Road Economic Belt and 21st Century Maritime Silk Road gives priority on facilities connectivity and unimpeded trade that explained the continuum development of the Social and Humane Philosophy of the Ideal Conception of the "Belt and Road Initiative" within the ambit of Maritime Silk Road.

Basically, the "Belt and Road Initiative" advocates the facilities connectivity as the priority areas of technical assistance for the Maritime Silk Road :

(1) The construction of international trunk passageways, and form an infrastructure network connecting all sub-regions in Asia, Africa and Europe.

(2) The transport infrastructure construction such as key passageways, junctions and projects, and give priority to linking up unconnected road sections, removing transport bottlenecks, advancing road safety facilities and traffic management facilities and equipment, and improving road network connectivity.

(3) The port infrastructure construction, build smooth land water transportation channels, and advance port cooperation; increase sea routes and the number of voyages, and enhance information technology cooperation in maritime logistics.

(4) The connectivity of energy infrastructure, work in concert to ensure the security of oil and gas pipelines and other transport routes, build cross-border power supply networks and power-transmission routes, and cooperate in regional power grid upgrading and transformation.

(5) The construction of cross-border optical cables and other communications trunk line networks, improve international communications connectivity, and create an Information Silk Road.

(6) The building bilateral cross-border optical cable networks at a quicker pace, plan transcontinental submarine optical cable projects, and improve spatial (satellite) information passageways to expand information exchanges and cooperation.

Trade and Investments

Investment and trade cooperation is a major task in building the "Belt and Road" that supports economic growth and development for all nations of the world. Other than the improvement of investment and trade facilitation to create a sound business environment including the mutual cooperation for international trade agreements. These are the important trade and investments needed to become dynamic and flexible in the manifestation of economic change and innovation:

1) The mutual investment areas, deepen cooperation in agriculture, forestry, animal husbandry and fisheries, agricultural machinery manufacturing and farm produce processing, and promote cooperation in marine-product farming, deep-sea fishing, aquatic product processing, seawater desalination, marine biopharmacy, ocean engineering technology, environmental protection industries, marine tourism and other fields.

2) The exploration and development of coal, oil, gas, metal minerals and other conventional energy sources; advance cooperation in hydropower, nuclear power, wind power, solar power and other clean, renewable energy sources; and promote cooperation in the processing and conversion of energy and resources at or near places where they are exploited, so as to create an integrated industrial chain of energy and resource cooperation.

3) The enhanced cooperation in deep processing technology, equipment and engineering services in the fields of energy and resources.

4) The cooperation of the emerging industries along new-generation information technology, biotechnology, new energy technology, new materials and other emerging industries, and establish entrepreneurial and investment cooperation mechanisms.

The significant contribution of the "Belt and Road Initiative" is the end product of its implementation of the infrastructure development. The huge economic investments in identifying the priority infrastructure support on the revival of the maritime silk road ensure the beneficial effects to human society.

B. Achieving the Development Philosophy of Freedom

The idea of freedom discusses the final continuum phase in the transformation of "Belt and Road Initiative" when achieved the change, innovation and idealism which represents the cycle of development. The quality of life depends on providing more on human needs and wants to transform the final action to achieve the desired development goals of a given society.

Furthermore, freedom is desecrated and corruptible without change and innovation. It will create government dependency and exploitation where engagements redounds in the human sufferings. The "Belt and Road Initiative" also provides technical infrastructure and technological innovation for the long run benefits in growth and development. In the Essence of Freedom, it does not mean the democratic ideals of the form of government when discussing the Essence of the " Belt and Road Initiative." This is the fourth continuum to identify the ladder of the economic development to fulfil the quality of life in the human society.

When do we achieve the Essence of Freedom of the "Belt and Road Initiative" in the Maritime Silk Road :

1. The human society is given an opportunity to participated the enabling and facilitating mechanism of the economic programs of the Maritime Silk Road.

2. The recipients of the economic programs are facilitated by the financial compensations and benefits for the participation of the long term activities of the "Belt and Road Initiative."

3. The long term economic impact justifies the creation of wealth and income including the employment generation given by the sustainable infrastructure investments and trade of the partner sovereign state.

4. The technical assistance of the infrastructure and investment support of the "Belt and Road Initiative" provides added economic value for all employed people in this program.

Thus, the existence of freedom ensures the full participation of the beneficiaries with direct or indirect economic impact in terms of financial assistance and grants . The freedom of enterprise demands the free flow of financial resources including good and services to achieve the full potential of the human civilization. The real worth of freedom must bring the people of the world to enjoy the fruits of their labor that will improve the quality of life. This is the real essence of freedom which must take into consider the value of social worth in bringing and satisfying the basic needs of the human society. They must have enough financial resources to spend the basic needs of life and enjoy the essence of life .

The technological development of the society particularly the introduction of internet in social media and matured commercial life demands the greater participation of the society to consume the economic goods for them to enjoy the full fruits of life. This can be translated by the demands of the tourism industries as the financial resources utilized by the tourists are their savings on income they receive in employment or business operation. However, the increasing number of unemployment and the presence of limited income may produce more of sufferings and exploitation particularly to the poor people who can barely produce what the family needs in terms of shelter, clothing, food and education for the children.

There can be no freedom when people suffers more on pains, frustrations and exploitations due to limit of their financial capability. The degree of freedom may not be present at all when poor people are in misery and exploited by those who have wealth and power. This is usually the consideration of quality of life when poverty alleviation has been reduce that can become the measurement of economic growth and development. The Marxist philosophy had been providing the essence of collective freedom when social equality justifies the humane life of all the human society.

Yet those who advocated the democratic principles of justice have not been able to identify the real meaning of freedom in the essence of life. You can live in highly democratic countries where all freedoms are unlimited in all forms of human activities as long as within the bounds of law. These are the social platforms on the highest degree of freedoms in the developed countries in the world. They highlights the human freedom from the political perspectives of democratic ideologies considered the most sacred respect of dignity and self-esteem with all men are equal and just in the fulfillment of humane society.

However, the world does not seemingly live what is expected to be equal and just when human beings are not given enough income to support their family. There are no jobs for them to get income and most of them live in misery. Even, they are employed and receiving monthly income for their salaries and wages the net home pay would not be enough to spend for their basic necessities such as food, shelter, clothing, education allowance and other miscellaneous expenses to live in decent life. In short, the salaries and wages received by the factory workers and laborers are considered as "poor people" who are within the poverty threshold line. This means that they cannot afford to buy or rent a decent shelter, cannot afford to buy food and taking three (3) meals a day, no allowance to support education, no extra saving to buy other basic necessities in life and other conditions of being classified as "poor." The contextual analysis of "state of being poor" from the point of view of "poverty" means no enough income to support the basic necessities of life such as food, shelter, clothing, education, health and other basic support to live in decent life.

The primary role of government is to deliver the basic services such as employment, education, health, environmental protection, security and safety which are considered as the social equity programs for those who are poor. These are the general and common welfare programs to fulfil in the Improvement of Quality of Life (IQL) particularly the underprivileged class that can result to decent life. However, the government programs are not enough to bring the decent life of the citizens as they need more income to support the family expenses on the basic necessities (food, shelter, clothing, education and health).

The social issues and challenges on low income and unemployment bring the catastrophic effects in the state of being "poor" particularly the famers, fishermen, labourer and factory workers. The social detriments that needed corrective actions of the economic developments in the eradication of poverty. Finally, the idea of freedom demands the full recognition and appreciation in the individuality that enough income of a family to provide a decent life. This has been the consideration in the political, economic and cultural development in the promotion of the human ideals of self-esteem, dignity and self-respect in the international community particularly the human development advocacy of the United Nations to reduce the poverty incidence in the sovereign states. If this will be achieved then we can say that lower class enjoys the highest degree of economic and political freedoms wherein the democratic ideals on the principles of equality and justice are well-enforced without prejudice from their self-esteem, dignity and respect to the highly stratified society.

Chapter VII
Accomplishments of the Maritime Silk Road Confucius Institute :
The Promotion of the Chinese Language and Culture
under the "Belt and Road Initiative"

Aiming to promote Chinese language and culture, Chinese government established Chinese National Office for Teaching Chinese as a Foreign Language (Hanban) to promote Chinese language and culture in September 27th, 2004. Up to now, 511 Confucius Institutes and 1,703 Confucius Classrooms have been established in 140 countries and regions. In 2016, the Confucius Institute and Classrooms around the world, with a team of 60, 000 Chinese and overseas full-time and part-time teachers, enrolled.

2.1 million students and hosted cultural events of various types, receiving a total of 13 million participants. In addition, 67 countries in the world include Chinese as their course and people learning Chinese reached 100,000,000 in the world (until December 15th, 2016)

Through the support of Hanban of Chinese teachers and resources, Thailand has established 15 Confucius Institutes and 11 Confucius Classrooms. Phraprommangkalachan, the founder of Confucius Classrooms, established the first Confucius Classrooms in the world and the named the new type of Confucius Institute "Maritime Silk Road Confucius Institute". Due to his great contribution to Chinese promotion and the communication between Chinese and Thai people, he gained awards in the 6th, 9th and 10th Confucius Institute Conference.

On the occasion of 10-year anniversary of the Confucius Institute, moving to the next decade, Phraprommangkalachan initiated the idea of establishing a new institute in order to widely promote the teaching and learning of Chinese language and culture. There would be a network with educational institutes, government offices, and private sector organizations where Chinese language was taught (not including 26 institutes and classrooms already in the network). This was to promote the teaching, training, and daily use of the language to reach the standard. Together with his group, Phraprommangkalachan asked to see Dr. Xu Lin, Director General of the Hanban, on October 10th 2014 at Hanban headquarters in Beijing. Dr. Xu Lin agreed to the idea of establishing the institute, and named it "Maritime Silk Road Confucius Institute". Tianjin Education Council was assigned to work together with the Maritime Silk Road Confucius Institute. Tianjin Education Council assigned Tianjin Normal University to work in partnership and appointed the Director of the Institute (Chinese counterpart) to work with the Director of the Institute

(Thai counterpart). The Institute is located at Dhurakij Pundit University and carries out the following duties under the administration of the board of Maritime Silk Road Confucius Institute:

- A non-profit public institution
- Chinese language teaching
- Training Native Thais teaching Chinese
- Organizing HSK examinations
- Providing the support and services of teaching resources
- Organizing activities to promote Chinese culture
- Organizing activities assigned by Hanban

Hanban will take these responsibilities:

- 150, 000 dollars initial capital
- Financial support for each year's projects
- 3000 books
- Chinese teachers

Dr. Xu Lin, Chief Executive of Confucius Institute Headquarters and Director General of Hanban, Phraprommangkalachan, President of Maritime Silk Road Confucius Institute and Associate Professor Dr. Varakorn Samakoses, President of Dhurakij Pundit University signed cooperative memorandum to establish Maritime Silk Road Confucius Institute in April 28th, 2015. In June 24th, 2015, Dr. Xu Lin awarded the plaque of the 14th Confucius Institute, Maritime Silk Road Confucius Institute to President Phraprommangkalachan and awarded the plaque of the first branch of Maritime Silk Road Confucius Institute to President of Dhurakij Pundit University. Except for the daily work, Maritime Silk Road Confucius Institute will also carry out these responsibilities:

- Promoting the Chinese teaching in the Vocational Education
- Developing the standardized Chinese teacher training
- Inviting the educational institutions, governmental institutions and social institutions associated with Chinese and Culture learning as the branch of Maritime Silk Road Confucius Institute, and improve the standard of Chinese usage.

In October 20th, 2015, Phraprommangkalachan, Hanban Thailand Officer and Mr. Zhou Gaoyu, First Secretary for Education, China Embassy visited the office of Maritime Silk Road Confucius Institute at Dhurakij Pundit University. In August 26th, 2015, Tianjin Normal University assigned He Bingzheng as the Chinese Dean of Maritime Silk Road Confucius Institute and Xiao Shan as the assistant of the Chinese

Dean to work together in the Confucius Institute. Dhurakij Pundit University and Tianjin Normal University will carry out the two responsibilities:

- Being The Secretary of Maritime Silk Road Confucius Institute
- The first branch of Maritime Silk Road Confucius Institute

Phraprommangkalachan is the president of Maritime Silk Road Confucius Institute, the President of the two universities will be the vice president of Maritime Silk Road Confucius Institute. In addition, the two Presidents will be the President of Maritime Silk Road Confucius Institute Dhurakij Pundit University Branch. The board of directors of Maritime Silk Road Confucius Institute are as follows

1.	Phraprommangkalachan	President
2.	Dr. Sathit Limpongpan	Vice President
3.	Associate professor Dr. Varakorn Samakoses	Vice President
4.	General Pinpart Sariwat	Board of Director
5.	Police Lieutenant General ML. Punsak Kasemsan	Board of Director
6.	Associate Professor Dr. Pranee Sangkhasap	Board of Director
7.	Associate Professor Dr. Chuangchot Pantuweat	Board of Director
8.	Associate Professor Dr. Issaree hunsacharoonroj	Board of Director
9.	Dr. Nilubol Limpongpan	Board of Director
10.	Dr. Darika Lathapipat	Board of Director
11.	Dr. Akanit Kangsang	Board of Director
12.	Mr. Wanchai Sornsiri	Board of Director
13.	Mr. Thanakorn Seriburi	Board of Director
14.	Mr. Niphon Chokphiromwongsa	Board of Director
15.	Mr. Rojana Kritcharoen	Board of Director
16.	Mr. Sansern Ngaorungsi	Board of Director
17.	Mr. Poonsak Pranootnarapam	Board of Director and Secretary
18.	Mr. Ekarat Janrathitikarn	Board of Director and Deputy Secretary
19.	Mr. He Bingzheng	Board of Director and Deputy Secretary

Signing memorandum of Exchange and Cooperation with 63 Institutions

Until December 15th, 2016

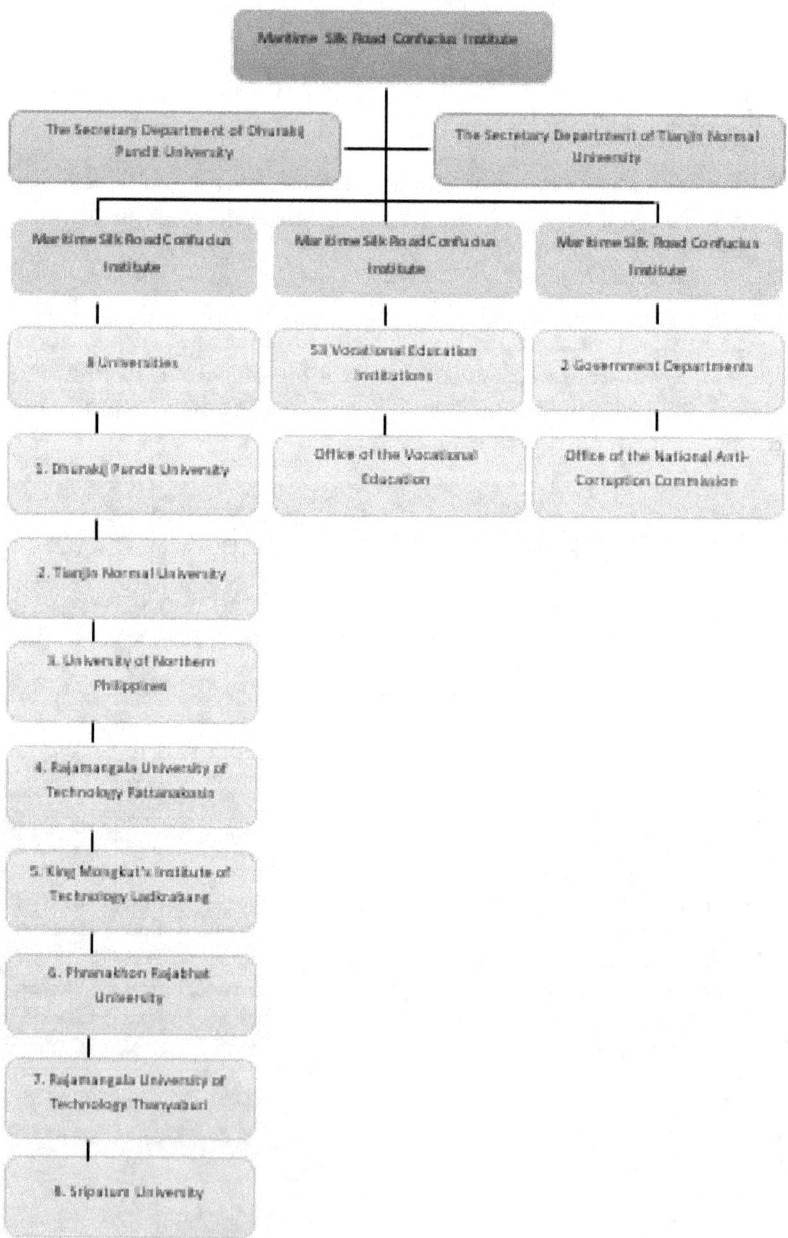

The Name List which have Signed Memorandum of Understanding with Maritime Silk Road Confucius Institute

Until December 15th, 2016, Maritime Silk Road Confucius Institute has signed Memorandum of Understanding with 8 universities, 2 government departments and 53 vocational institutions.

Report of Maritime Silk Road Confucius Institute

1. On August 26th, 2016, Maritime Silk Road Confucius Institute signed MOU with Office of the National Anti-Corruption Commission and completed the Chinese training of 2 groups, a total of 40 officers in the National Anti-Corruption Commission. One of the groups studied in Tianjin Normal University in March, 2016 and it costs a total of 500, 000 Baht.

2. In the support of People's Government of Tianjin Educational Commission, 3 groups, a total of 49 vocational educational education students studied in China for 3 years with scholarships (Chinese training and vocational education), costing a total of 27, 624,240 Baht (scholarship 34, 800 CNY/year x 3 years x 49 students)

3. In November, 2015, we organized 4 Thai Teaching Chinese to further Chinese training in Tianjin for 15 days with total cost of 20, 000 baht.

4. We organized a cultural exchange program between China and Thailand. Hainan Province Office of Education cooperated with Nawamintharachinuthit Horwang Nonthaburi School, Benjamarachanusorn World Class Standard School and Suankularbwittayalai Nonthaburi School. China and Thailand, each selected 50 teachers and students for visit exchange from October to November in 2015.

5. From March 5th to march 20th, 2016, Thailand Chinese Culture Center, Tourism Authority of Thailand and Thailand China Tourism Association trained Chinese language for 50 tourist guides.

6. TianjinEducation Commission discussed with Phranakhon Si Ayuthaya Technical College about "Luban Workshop". On the 8th of March, 2016, they held the inauguration ceremony with total cost of 15, 350,000 Baht.

7. On June 30th, 2016, we signed MoU with Thailand Juvenile and Family Court. We trained Chinese for the staff and jury members of the court, a total of 120 people, from June, 18th to July 30th, 2016.

8. We signed MoU with 63 universities and vocational educational colleges.

9. The 13th "Chinese Language Bridge-Top Crown Diamond Cup" international Chinese Language Competition was held in September 4th, at in Dhurakij Pundit University. 3,577 participants took part in this competition, which total cost of 1,800,000 Baht.

10. Hanban approved the application for the setting up of HSK test center at Maritime Silk Road Confucius Institute; it will be held at Dhurakij Pundit University and other cooperative institutions in 2017.

11. On September 22nd, 2016, we held the activity of Mid-Autumn Festival. We introduced the culture of Mid-Autumn Festival to the teachers and students of Dhurakij Pundit University. A total of 200 students took part in this event.

12. From September 26th to 29th, 2016, under the support of CP Group and HNA Group and Hainan Airline, Phraprommangkalachan and the Education Department of Hainan Province, the board of directors of Maritime Silk Road Confucius Institute, 5 Thai Universities (Navamindradhiraj University, King Mongkut's Institute of Technology Ladkrabang, Rajamangala University of Technology Thanyaburi, Siam University and Dhurakij Pundit University) and 9 universities from Hainan Province held meetings and signed 21 MOU. They reached agreements about teacher and student exchange programs in January and February of 2017. Master Yinshun invited Phraprommangkalachan as the Guest Professor of The Buddhism Accademy of Nanhai. The Chairman of the Board of Hainan Airline, Wang Jian presented letter of appointment to Phraprommangkalachan as Guest Professor of Sanya Aviation & Tourism College.

13. On September 29th, 2016, we participated in the Reception of Chinese National Day in Shangri-La Hotel.

14. We organize the work of Chinese teaching for 11 subjects in the Chinese business major of Dhurakij Pundit University (DPU). At the same time, we undertook 2 basic Chinese training courses.

15. From December 9th to 11th, 2016, we attended the 11th Confucius Institute Conference in Kunming and prepared for the project of 2017.On December 10th, 2016, at 16:45, the President of Maritime Silk Road Confucius Institute, Phraprommangkalachan led the members of the board to meet Hao Ping, the Vice Minister of Education. They discussed how to produce teaching materials meeting the demand of Thailand primary schools, high schools, Vocational College and University in addition, maritime Silk Road Confucius believed that if the Chinese volunteer teachers of primary school and high school mastered Thai language and culture, it would be an advantage for Chinese teaching. Thus, they discussed about the training of Thai language and culture for Chinese volunteer teachers.

16. On December 13th, 2016 Dali University signed implementation agreement with Phranakhon Rajabhat University to establish the second branch of maritime Silk Road Confucius Institute.

The Achievements (Accomplishments) of Maritime Silk Road Confucius Institute from January to December of 2016 are as follows:

1. Developing Chinese textbooks

The institute is currently working together with Tianjin Normal University and 4 leading universities on the project. The Confucius Institute has proposed 10 universities and 10 schools in all regions of Thailand as institutes responsible for examining the curriculum and textbooks.

2. Promoting tourism

In cooperation with Department of tourism and Thai-Chinese tourism alliance association, the institute provided workshops for 50 Mandarin speaking tour guides at the Chinese Cultural Center from 5 to 20 March 2016.

3. Teaching and learning support at the university level

3.1 The institute provided China Scholarship Council scholarships (CSC scholarship) 1 scholarship for doctoral study and 5 scholarships for master's degree. The six scholarships are worth a total of 4, 400, 000 Baht.

3.2 The institute provided 9 Hanban scholarships for master's degree. The scholarships are worth a total of 5, 400, 000 baht.

3.3 Executives from the 5 institutes attended a conference and signed a Memorandum of Understanding (MoU) with the Education Department and 9 universities in Hainan, People's Republic of China from 26th to 29th September 2016. It is expected that there will be student/teacher exchange programs and mutual research projects from January-February 2017 onwards. This project was supported by HNA Group and CP Group, valued at 1,000,000 Baht

3.4 The institute initiated a Chinese Camp project for the Chinese program, Faculty of Arts, Dhurakij Pundit University. The project allowed 19 students and 1 teacher to study at Tianjin Normal University for 15 days-scheduled after 20th December 2016. The students were responsible only for their own airfare. No expenses were charged to the teacher. The scholarships are worth a total of 1,000,000 baht.

4. Teaching and learning support in vocational and technical education.

4.1 The Secretary-General of the Office of the Vocational Education Commission, the executives, and directors from about 15 colleges attended a conference and signed a Memorandum of Understanding (MoU) with Tianjin Education Council in September 2014.

4.2 The institute received scholarships for high-level vocational education institutions from The Tianjin Education Council. The scholarships are for vocational students 15 scholarships for 5 consecutive years. Each scholarship is worth 563,760 baht for 3 year study (for language learning and for high vocational education). The scholarships are worth a total of 42,282,000 baht (15 scholarships x 563,760 baht x 5 years). Until now, the scholarships have been granted to two batches, (30 students in each).

4.3 The institute obtained 20 scholarships from Tianjin People's Representative assembly for vocational education. The scholarships are worth 563,760 each for 3-year study, and worth a total of 11,275,200 baht. The students who won the scholarships left the country for their study on 25th October 2016.

4.4 Tianjin Education Council supported the institute in establishing Luban Institute of Skills Development, which is worth 15,350,000 baht, at Ayutthaya Technical College. (Ayutthaya Technical College cooperated with Bohai Vocational Technical College) The opening ceremony was on 8 March 2016.

4.5 Vocational student exchange between Thai and Chinese colleges in MoU has taken place in 3 scholarship batches, 30 students and 2 teachers each. The scholarships are for 3 months each. The scholarships are worth 907,500 baht each, a total of 2,722,500 baht.

4.6 Ayutthaya Technical College is now coordinating with Tianjin Bohai Vocational Technical College in creating smart classrooms, each measuring 8 x 16 meters, which are worth a total of 1.2 million baht.

4.7 The institute signed a Memorandum of Understanding (MoU) with Office of the Vocational Education Commission and 53 vocational colleges.

5. Teaching and learning support in vocational and technical education.

5.1 Chinese volunteer teachers organized Chinese language and cultural activities for schools; Suankularb Wittayalai Nonthaburi, for example.

5.2 The institute initiated The Exchange Thai-Chinese language and culture Program between Hainan Educational Service Area and Nawamit Tarachi Nuthit Howang, Nonthaburi School. The program provided opportunities for Thai-Chinese cultural exchange to 50 teachers and students from each party.

5.3 The institute supplied two scholarships for high school education and two scholarships for Chinese language learning. The four scholarships are worth a total of 1,500,000 baht.

6. Training for Chinese volunteer teachers.

The institute considers that some volunteer teachers still lack sufficient experience in teaching and also an understanding of Thai customs and traditions which are different in each part of Thailand. Therefore, it offers a one-month training course to all Chinese volunteer teachers prior to commencement of work. The institute is currently waiting for the approval from the headquarter. However, Dhurakij Pundit University, as the Secretariat of Confucius Institute, regularly provides training and has 6 Chinese volunteer teachers study Thai customs and traditions.

7. Chinese language training for government officers

7.1 The institute signed a Memorandum of Understanding (MoU) with Office of the national Anti-Corruption Commission in August 26, 2016. Chinese language training was provided for two batches, each consisting of 40 participants. Scholarships were granted to one batch of 15 participants for further study of the Chinese language and culture in Tianjin in March 2016. The scholarships are worth 500,000 baht.

7.2 The institute signed a Memorandum of Understanding (MoU) with Central Juvenile and Family Court. Chinese language training was provided to 120 participants-associate judges, government officers, and staff members

8. Providing services for other affiliates at Maritime Silk Road Confucius Institute

8.1 As a number of universities proposed to become the affiliates of maritime Silk Road Confucius Institutes, the institute organized two meetings in order to inform the policies and guidelines for cooperation. The first meeting was with The Office of the Vocational Education Commission and 53 vocational colleges on 14 March 2016 at Dhurakij Pundit University.

8.2 The two branches that signed agreement with Maritime Silk Road Confucius Institute. The first branch, Dhurakij Pundit University, cooperated with Tianjin Normal University.The second branch, Phranakhon Rajabhat University, Cooperated with Dali University.

9. As a HSK test center

9. The institute has been authorized by the Institute Headquarters to be a HSK test center from January 2017 onwards. The first test date is scheduled for February 2017 in two days:

1. Dhurakij Pundit University as the test venue.

2. The test venues outside Dhurakij Pundit University with the cooperation from:

2.1 The networking institutes

2.2 20 Dhurakij Pundit University's sister schools where Chinese language is taught

2.3 11 schools where Confucius Classrooms are based

10. Expansion of Maritime Silk Road Confucius Institute to ASEAN

10.1 The University of Northern Philippines has an interest shown to become an affiliate of Maritime Silk Road Confucius Institute

10.2 The institute is currently planning to travel to Myanmar, Vietnam, and Malaysia

11. Diamond on the Top of the Crown Project

The institute organized the Chinese language competition, the 13th Diamond on the Top Crown project (International) on 4th September 2016 at Dhurakij Pundit University. This Chinese language competition was at all levels (5 levels), with 3,577 student competitors. The budget for the competition and the prizes was 1,800,000 baht.

12. Establishment of Confucius Institute Alumni Association

The instate now has the name list of students who have received the scholarships from Hanban, the Institute Headquarter. On the list are now 109 names. The list will be posted on the institute's website in the near future. The institute is now in the process of requesting permission for the establishment of Confucius Institute Alumni Association.

13. Cultural Exchange Program

13.1 The institute and Romchatra Foundation consider that 28 paintings on the topic of "Civilization of Maritime Silk Road", displayed in the Diamond on the Top of the Crown Art Contest 2015 at the National Gallery on Chao Fa Rd. in Bangkok, demonstrate the relationship of the Republic of China with Southeast Asia, South Asia, Western Asia, Africa and Europe. President Xi Jinping stated that Southeast Asia is one important economic zone for the maritime Silk Road. Therefore, the institute has sent the letter requesting the venue for the exhibitions "Maritime Silk Road in the eyes of Thailand Artist" on 14 January- 7 February 2017 at Chinese Cultural Center in Thailand.

13.2 Maritime Silk Road Confucius Institute held different kinds of activities in Dhurakij Pundit University and other primary schools and high schools, including Chinese calligraphy, paper cutting, martial arts, weiqi, making dumplings and playing Chinese instrument.

General Situation of Confucius Institute in Thailand

Hanban/Confucius Institute Headquarters, as a public institution affiliated with the Chinese Ministry of education, is committed to providing Chinese language and cultural teaching resources and services worldwide, it goes all out in meeting the demands of foreign Chinese learners and contributing to the development of multiculturalism and the building of a harmonious world. The Hanban describes itself as a "non-government and non-profit organization". The Confucius Institutes was established across the world to teach Chinese. The Head of the Confucius Institute is located in Beijing, People's Republic of China.

After 2005, Confucius Institute and Confucius Classroom were established around the world. Confucius Institute are built in universities and Confucius Classrooms are built in middle schools. Hanban selects and dispatches Chinese directors and teaching staff to Confucius Institutes every year. Up to now, 511 Confucius Institute and 1,073 Confucius Classrooms have been established in 140 countries and regions. (Until December 15th, 2016).

Confucius Institute is named after the famous Chinese philosopher, Confucius. He was the great Chinese teacher, editor, politician, and philosopher in Chinese history. The philosophy of Confucius has a great influence around the world. Thus, Confucius Institute expresses the board and profound Chinese culture and the inheritance of Chinese culture.

The Organizational Structure of Confucius Institute are as follows:

1) Confucius Institute Headquarters, a non-profit organization;

2) The Council of Confucius Institute Headquarters. The president, vice president and permanent members will be appointed by the Chinese government and 33 members will be appointed by the country's Confucius Institute.

3) The secretariat of Confucius Institute belongs to The Council of Confucius Institute Headquarters. The director General of Hanban is the Chief Executive.

4) Functions of Confucius Institute Headquarters:

4.1 To organize annual Confucius Institute conferences.

1.2 To make development plans and set down establishment and evaluation criterion for Confucius Institutes.

1.3 To examine, approve and establish Confucius Institutes.

1.4 To examine and approve annual project proposals, budgets and financial statements of Confucius Institute worldwide.

1.5 To provide Confucius Institute around the world with the support and services of teaching resources.

4.6 To select and dispatch Chinese directors and teaching staff to Confucius Institutes, and to offer training programs for the management teams and teachers of Confucius Institutes.

An application for the permission to establish a Confucius Institute must satisfactorily demonstrate the following:

1) That the applicant is legally registered organization or corporation at the place where it is located with resources to conduct teaching, educational and cultural exchanges, and public service;

2) That there is a demand for learning the Chinese language and culture at the applicant's location;

3) That the personnel, space, facilities, and equipment required for language and culture instruction are available;

4) That the capital for the establishment is in place, and that the source of funds for operation is stable.

Before applying for the establishment of Confucius institute, the applying institution should apply for the Chinese executive institution and sign an agreement and submit it to Confucius Institute Headquarters. Upon the approval of an application, the Confucius Institute Headquarters will sign an agreement with the applicant. At last, the Chinese executive institution as a representative of Hanban will sign an agreement of establishment of the Confucius Institute with the applicant. Confucius Institute Headquarters will confer the permission for establishment and the official Confucius Institute Plaque upon that applicant. Generally, there are English and Chinese on the plaque, but the Confucius Institute in Thailand add Thai language on the plaque. Before the inauguration ceremony, an awarding plaque ceremony of the Confucius institute will be held.

The name list of Confucius Institute in Thailand are as follows:

1) Confucius Institute at Khon Kaen University-Southwest University
2) Confucius Institute at Mae Fah Luang University-Xiamen University
3) Confucius Institute at Chiang Mai University-Yunnan Normal University
4) Confucius Institute at Bansomdejchaopraya Rajabhat University-Tianjin Normal University
5) Confucius Institute at Phuket, Prince of Songkla University-Shanghai University
6) Confucius Institute at Mahasarakham University-Guangxi University for Nationalities
7) Confucius Institute of Suan Dusit University at Suphanbui-Guangxi University
8) Confucius Institute of Betong Municipality-Chongqing University
9) Confucius Institute at Prince of Songkla University-Guangxi Normal University
10) Confucius Institute at Chulalongkorn University- Peking University
11) Confucius Institute at Kasetsart University-Huaqiao University
12) Confucius Institute at Burapha Universit Wenzhou University, Wenzhou Medical University
13) Confucius Institute at Assumption University-Tianjin University of Science & Technology

Maritime Silk Road Confucius Institute at Dhurakij Pundit University-Tianjin Normal Normal University

14) Chinese Medical Confucius Institute at Huachiew Chalermprakiet university-Tianjin Medical University.

The chairman and vice-chairman should be the president of Thai University or the president of Chinese University in turn every other year. Both the Thai Executive Director and the Chinese Executive Director should execute the decision made by the board and holding responsibility to the board. The Confucius Institute should implement the following works according to the rules of Confucius Institute Headquarters:
1) Chinese language teaching;
2) Training Chinese language instructors and providing Chinese language teaching resources;

3) Holding the HSK examination (Chinese Proficiency Test) and test for the Certification of the Chinese Language Teachers;
4) Providing information and consultative services concerning China's education, culture, and so forth;
5) Conducting language and cultural exchange activities between China and other countries.

Expenses and use of budgets of the Confucius Institute:
1) Hanban will provide 150,000 USD as the initial fund of every Confucius institute
2) Hanban will provide project funds to projects applied by Confucius Institute
3) The funds of the Institute will be deposited in the Institute's special account in the commercial bank and will be used independently. The Confucius institute should send budget application to Hanban every year before Jan 15th.

The name list of Confucius classroom in Thailand are as follows:
1) Confucius Classroom at Traimit Wittayalai High School
2) Confucius Classroom at Suankularb Wittayalai School
3) Confucius Classroom at Nawamintharachinuthid Horwang Nonthaburi School
4) Confucius Classroom at Lampang Kanlayanee School
5) Confucius Classroom at Rayong Wittayakorn School
6) Confucius Classroom at Phuket Wittayalai School
7) Confucius Classroom at Chltralada School
8) Confucius Classroom at Xingmin School Chiangmai
9) Confucius Classroom at Swang Boriboon Witaya School Chonburi
10) Confucius Classroom at Srinakorn School Songkla
11) Confucius Classroom at Assumption Commercial School

Chapter VIII
"Belt and Road Initiative" of the Maritime Silk Road Confucius Institute for World Peace and Development by President Xi Jinping of China

The keynote speech given by Chinese President Xi Jinping at the Boa Forum for Asia Annual Conference 2015 with the theme Towards a Community of Common Destiny and A New Future for Asia last March 28, 2015 has provided important insights in the paradigm shift model of the "Belt and Road Initiative" for the development strategies for Asia and the world. The historical importance of the "Belt and Road Initiative" has been successfully done by this peaceful navigational trade that existed in the Asian nations which can now revived the existence of world peace and development in the Maritime Silk Road Initiative :
(http://www.fmprc.gov.cn/mfa_eng/wjdt_665385/zyjh_665391/t1250690.shtml)

> *" The timing could not be better in that the theme has not only great immediate relevance but also long-term historical significance. And I am looking to all of you to express yourselves fully and contribute your insightful views to the cause of peace and development of Asia and beyond"*

In the case of the Asian region, President Xi Jinping reminded the people of what happened in the past in the World Anti—Fascist War but the reflection of the peace in Asia must look into the future. He also mentioned that the world has experienced profound changes as never before, making a difference to the destiny of mankind with the days of global colonialism and the Cold War long gone. He now set the paradigm shift of the idea of World Peace and Development in his Maritime Silk Road through the "Belt and Road Initiative" as to the existence of the sovereign nations though amity and comity. This defines on oneness and closeness of the people of the world for peaceful co-existence to promote political and economic freedom will bring the much needed service for common welfare in the achievement of quality of life for all. This is important to the social and economic development that transforms the Asian society at a higher level degree of freedom. In this sense, the Asian nations will bring new era of world peace where the criteria of freedom revolves in the development of self-esteem, recognition, dignity and self-respect as a consequence of the embracing the implementation of "Belt and Road. Initiative"

These are the highlights of President Xi Jinping initiative in the paradigm shift of the World Peace and Development in "Belt and Road Initiative : "

1. **Interdependence and Interconnection**. According to President Xi Jinping, the nations of the world are working for interconnection and interdependence to achieve peace and development in the region. This paradigm shift provides peace, development and win-win cooperation which have become the prevailing trend of our times. The international forces are shifting in a way that is more favorable to maintain world peace. Countries are now in a better position to uphold general stability in the world and seek common development.

2. **Regional Cooperation**. The diplomatic strategy in this component has the features of mutual respect, consensus-building and accommodation. As he said in the conference that after gaining national independence, Asian countries will take their destiny in their own hands and will strengthen the force for regional and world peace. Asian countries were the first to advocate the Five (5) Principles of Peaceful Co-existence and, together with African countries, put forward the Ten Principles on handling state-to-state relations at the Bandung Conference. Likewise, he mentioned that the Asian countries have gradually come up with an Asian way of cooperation in the course of advancing regional cooperation, which features mutual respect, consensus-building and accommodation of each other's comfort levels. All these have contributed to a proper approach to state-to-state relations and progress in building a new type of international relations.

3. **Connectivity and Economic Growth.** This presents in the ensuring their own development paths to fast-track the economic growth to reduce poverty and backwardness development which has been done through faster interconnectivity, and inter-regional cooperation. The Asian countries became the most successful regions in the world that achieve this economic development and prosperity. It accounted to one third of the world economy, and Asia is one of the most dynamic regions with the most potential and its global strategic importance has been rising.

4. **Diplomatic Strategy of Openness and Inclusiveness.** The differences in ideology and social system are no longer the hindrance in international diplomacy where the interest of Asian countries and the rest of the world have become intertwined and a community of common destiny has increasingly taken shape. This is the diplomatic result of openness and inclusiveness where trust and appreciation must be implemented among the nations of the world. These are the international issues and challenges that must be addressed to bring peaceful cooperation among nations to work hand on hand in any world debacles such as international financial crisis, devastating disasters, and international historical disputes. The most important is to grow the economy, improve people's livelihood and eliminate poverty.

5. **Great Vision of Statemen to Support Peace and Development.** The contribution of peace and development of the outstanding leader and statemen like Mr. Lee Kuan Yew earned respect in Asia. The great vision of the leader reflects the kind of cooperation and exchanges in the rest of the world.

These are the following highlights of the message of President Xi Jinping on the paradigm shift for peace and development to further analyze the current issues and challenges that must be addressed to embrace the new future that will seek progress and development in tandem with that of the world.

1. The international situation continues to experience profound and complex changes, with significant development in multipolarization and economic globalization.

2. Cultural diversity and IT application are making constant progress while readjustment is accelerating in international landscape and order.

3. Countries around the world are losing no time in adjusting their development strategies, pursuing transformation and innovation, changing their economic development models, improving economic structures and opening up new horizons for further development.

4. The world economy is still in a period of profound adjustment, with risks of low growth, low inflation and low demand interwoven with risks of high unemployment, high debt and high level of bubbles. The

performance and policies of major economies continue to diverge, and uncertainties in the economic climate remain prominent.

5.   Geopolitical factors are more at play and local turmoil's keep cropping up. Non-traditional security threats and global challenges including terrorism, cyber security, energy security, food security, climate change and major infectious diseases are on the rise, and the North-South gap is still wide.

Furthermore, President Xi Jinping has given the genuine opportunity to embrace the "Belt and Road Initiative" through the Maritime Silk Road which advocated the noble cause of peace and development remains a long and arduous journey for mankind.

> *We have only one planet, and countries share one world. To do well, Asia and the world could not do without each other. Facing the fast changing international and regional landscapes, we must see the whole picture, follow the trend of our times and jointly build a regional order that is more favorable to Asia and the world. We should, through efforts towards such a community for Asia, promote a community of common interest for all mankind.*

These are exact thoughts and vision for shared opportunity to work as advocated by of President Xi Jinping in the quest for Peace and Development through "Belt and Road Initiative" in the Maritime Silk Road:

1.   **To build a community of common destiny, we need to make sure that all countries respect one another and treat each other as equals.**

Countries may differ in size, strength or level of development, but they are all equal members of the international community with equal rights to participate in regional and international affairs. On matters that involve us all, we should discuss and look for a solution together. Being a big country means shouldering greater responsibilities for regional and world peace and development, as opposed to seeking greater monopoly over regional and world affairs. To respect one another and treat each other as equals, countries need to, first and foremost, respect other countries' social systems and development paths of their own choice, respect each other's core interests and major concerns and have objective and rational perception of other countries' growing strength, policies and visions. Efforts should be made to seek common ground while shelving differences, and better still to increase common interests and dissolve differences. The hard-won peace and stability in Asia and the sound momentum for development should be upheld by all. All of us must oppose interference in other countries' internal affairs and reject attempts to destabilize the region out of selfish motives.

2. To build a community of common destiny, we need to seek win-win cooperation and common development.

Our friends in Southeast Asia say that the lotus flowers grow taller as the water rises. Our friends in Africa say that if you want to go fast, walk alone; and if you want to go far, walk together. Our friends in Europe say that a single tree cannot block the chilly wind. And Chinese people say that when big rivers have water, the small ones are filled; and when small rivers have water, the big ones are filled. All these sayings speak to one same truth, that is, only through win-win cooperation can we make big and sustainable achievements that are beneficial to all. The old mindset of zero-sum game should give way to a new approach of win-win and all-win cooperation. The interests of others must be accommodated while pursuing one's own interests, and common development must be promoted while seeking one's own development. The vision of win-win cooperation not only applies to the economic field, but also to the political, security, cultural and many other fields. It not only applies to countries within the region, but also cooperation with countries from outside the region. We should enhance coordination of macroeconomic policies to prevent negative spill-over effects that may arise from economic policy changes in individual economies. We should actively promote reform of global economic governance, uphold an open world economy, and jointly respond to risks and challenges in the world economy.

China and ASEAN countries will join hands in building an even closer China-ASEAN community of common destiny. The building of an East Asia economic community for ASEAN, China, Japan and ROK will be completed in 2020. We should actively build a free trade cooperation network in Asia and strive to conclude negotiations on an upgraded China-ASEAN FTA and on Regional Comprehensive Economic Partnership (RCEP) in 2015. In advancing economic integration in Asia, we need to stay committed to open regionalism and move forward trans-regional cooperation, including APEC, in a coordinated manner. We will vigorously promote a system of regional financial cooperation, explore a platform for exchanges and cooperation among Asian financial institutions, and advance complementary and coordinated development between the Asian Infrastructure Investment Bank (AIIB) and such multilateral financial institutions as the Asian Development Bank and the World Bank. We will strengthen practical cooperation in currency stability, investment and financing, and credit rating, make progress in institution building for the Chiang Mai Initiative Multilateralization and build a regional financial security network. We will work towards an energy and resources cooperation mechanism in Asia to ensure energy and resources security.

China proposes that plans be formulated regarding connectivity building in East Asia and Asia at large to advance full integration in infrastructure, policies and institutions and personnel flow. We may increase maritime connectivity, speed up institution building for marine cooperation in Asia, and step up cooperation in marine economy, environmental protection, disaster management and fishery. This way, we could turn the seas of Asia into seas of peace, friendship and cooperation for Asian countries.

3. **To build a community of common destiny, we need to pursue common, comprehensive, cooperative and sustainable security.**

In today's world, security means much more than before and its implications go well beyond a single region or time frame. All sorts of factors could have a bearing on a country's security. As people of all countries share common destiny and become increasingly interdependent, no country could have its own security ensured without the security of other countries or of the wider world. The Cold War mentality should truly be discarded and new security concepts be nurtured as we explore a path for Asia that ensures security for all, by all and of all.

We believe that countries are all entitled to take an equal part in regional security affairs and all are obliged to work to ensure security for the region. The legitimate security concerns of each country need to be respected and addressed. At the same time, in handling security issues in Asia, itis important to bear in mind both the history and reality of Asia, take a multi-pronged and holistic approach, improve coordinated regional security governance, and safeguard security in both the traditional and non-traditional realms. It is important to conduct dialogue and cooperation to enhance security at national and regional levels, and to increase cooperation as the way to safeguard peace and security. It is important to resolve disputes through peaceful means, and oppose the willful use or threat of force. Security should be given equal emphasis as development, and sustainable development surely provides a way to sustainable security. Countries in Asia need to step up cooperation with countries and organizations outside the region and all parties are welcome to play a positive and constructive role in upholding development and security in Asia.

4. To build a community of common destiny, we need to ensure inclusiveness and mutual learning among civilizations.

History, over the past millennia, has witnessed ancient civilizations appear and thrive along the Yellow and Yangtze Rivers, the Indus, the Ganges, the Euphrates, and the Tigris River as well as in Southeast Asia, each adding its own splendor to the progress of human civilization. Today, Asia has proudly maintained its distinct diversity and still nurtures all the civilizations, ethnic groups and religions in this big Asian family.

According to President Xi Jinping, he expounded the view of broad-based cooperation and dialogue to achieve the vision of " Belt and Road Initiative" as he compared the great philosophers of China who have provided the strong foundation of inter-civilization exchanges that promoted the peace of the world which can be applied in the ideas of international cooperation based on the ideas of mutual learning and common development to all.

Mencius, the great philosopher in ancient China, said, "Things are born to be different. "Civilizations are only unique, and no one is superior to the other. There is a need to have more exchange and dialogue among civilizations and development models, so that each could draw on the strength of the other and all could thrive and prosper by way of mutual learning and common development. Let us promote inter-civilization exchanges to build bridges of friendship for our people, drive human development and safeguard peace of the world.

China proposes that a conference of dialogue among Asian civilizations be held to provide a platform upon which to enhance interactions among the youth, people's groups, local communities and the media and to form a network of think-tank cooperation, so as to add to Asian people's rich cultural life and contribute to more vibrant regional cooperation and development.

The implementation of the development vision of "Belt and Road Initiative" through the Maritime Silk Road has reaffirmed China's commitment to the path of peaceful development in promoting cooperation and common development in the Asia -Pacific :

1. The Chinese people are working in unison under the strategic plans to complete the building of a moderately prosperous society in all respects, and to comprehensively deepen reform, advance law-based governance, and enforce strict Party conduct. Our objective is to realize the "two centenary" goals for China's development and for realizing the Chinese dream of great national rejuvenation. China will be firm in its determination and resolve and all its policies will be designed to achieve such a purpose.

2. The Chinese economy has entered a state of new normal. It is shifting gear from high speed to medium-to-high speed growth, from an extensive model that emphasized scale and speed to a more intensive one emphasizing quality and efficiency, and from being driven by investment in production factors to being driven by innovation.

    China's economy grew by 7.4% in 2014, with 7% increase in labor productivity and 4.8% decrease in energy intensity. The share of domestic consumption in GDP rose, the services sector expanded at a faster pace, and the economy's efficiency and quality continued to improve. When looking at China's economy, one should not focus on growth rate only. As the economy continues to grow in size, around 7% growth would be quite impressive, and the momentum it generates would be larger than growth at double digits in previous years. It is fair to say that the Chinese economy is highly resilient and has much potential, which gives us enough room to leverage a host of policy tools. Having said that, China will continue to be responsive to the new trend and take initiatives to shape the new normal in our favor. We will focus on improving quality and efficiency, and give even greater priority to shifting the growth model and adjusting the structure of development. We will make more solid efforts to boost economic development and deepen reform and opening-up. We will take more initiatives to unleash the creativity and ingenuity of the people, be more effective in safeguarding equity and social justice, raise people's living standards and make sure that China's economic and social development are both sound and stable.

3. This new normal of the Chinese economy will continue to bring more opportunities of trade, growth, investment and cooperation for other countries in Asia and beyond.

    In the coming five years, China will import more than US$10 trillion of goods, Chinese investment abroad will exceed US$500 billion, and more than 500 million outbound visits will be made by Chinese tourists. China will stick to its basic state policy of opening up, improve its investment climate, and protect the lawful rights and interests of investors. I believe that together, the people of Asian countries could drive this train of Asia's development to take Asia to an even brighter future.

4. What China needs most is a harmonious and stable domestic environment and a peaceful and tranquil international environment. Turbulence or war runs against the fundamental interests of the Chinese people. The Chinese nation loves peace and has, since ancient times, held high such philosophies that "harmony is the most valuable", "peace and harmony should prevail" and "all men under heaven are brothers".

    China has suffered from turbulence and war for more than a century since modern times, and the Chinese people would never want to inflict the same tragedy on other countries or peoples. History has taught us that no country who tried to achieve its goal with force ever succeeded. China will be steadfast in pursuing the independent foreign policy of peace, the path of peaceful development, the win-win strategy of opening-up, and the approach of upholding justice while pursuing shared interests. China will work to promote a new type of international relations of win-win cooperation and will always remain a staunch force for world peace and common development.

5. Close neighbors are better than distant relatives. This is a simple truth that the Chinese people got to know in ancient times. That explains China's firm commitment to building friendship and

partnership with its neighbors to foster an amicable, secure and prosperous neighborhood.

Under the principle of amity, sincerity, mutual benefit and inclusiveness, China is working actively to deepen win-win cooperation and connectivity with its neighbors to bring them even more benefit with its own development. China has signed treaties of good-neighborliness, friendship and cooperation with eight of its neighbors and is holding discussion to sign a same treaty with ASEAN. China stands ready to sigh such a treaty with all its neighbors to provide strong support for the development of bilateral relations as well as prosperity and stability in the region.

In 2013, during my visit to Kazakhstan and Indonesia, I put forward the initiatives of building a Silk Road economic belt and a 21st century maritime Silk Road. The "Belt and Road" initiative, meeting the development needs of China, countries along the routes and the region at large, will serve the common interests of relevant parties and answer the call of our time for regional and global cooperation.

In promoting this initiative, China will follow the principle of wide consultation, joint contribution and shared benefits. The programs of development will be open and inclusive, not exclusive. They will be a real chorus comprising all countries along the routes, not a solo for China itself. To develop the Belt and Road is not to replace existing mechanisms or initiatives for regional cooperation. Much to the contrary, we will build on the existing basis to help countries align their development strategies and form complementarity. Currently, more than 60 countries along the routes and international organizations have shown interest in taking part in the development of the Belt and the Road. The "Belt and Road" and the AIIB are both open initiatives. We welcome all countries along the routes and in Asia, as well as our friends and partners around the world, to take an active part in these endeavors.

Furthermore, the "Belt and Road Initiative" is not meant as rhetoric. It represents real work that could be seen and felt to bring real benefits to countries in the region. Thanks to the concerted efforts of relevant parties, the vision and action paper of the initiative has been developed. Substantive progress has been made in the establishment of the AIIB. The Silk Road Fund has been launched, and constructions of a number of infrastructure connectivity projects are moving forward. These early harvests have truly pointed to the broad prospects the "Belt and Road Initiative " will bring.

The cause of peace and development of mankind is as lofty as it is challenging. The journey ahead will not be smooth sailing, and success may not come easy. No matter how long and difficult the journey may be, those who work together and never give up will eventually prevail. I believe that as long as we keep to our goals and make hard efforts, we will together bring about a community of common destiny and usher in a new future for Asia.

Chapter IX
Unifying Universal Perspectives of Change, Innovation, Idealism and Freedom : The Strategic Direction and Opportunity of " Belt and Road Initiative"

The blueprint of the Maritime Silk Road Initiative on "Belt and Road Initiative" for World Peace and Development by Chinese President Xi Jinping of China has extensively identified the common ground on the strategic implementation of this program. This chapter justifies the paradigm shift of World Peace and Development through the development mechanism on change, innovation, idealism and freedom.

Development Mechanisms in the Paradigm Shift of World Peace and Development

The highlights of President Xi Jinping on "Belt and Road Initiative" represent the broad range of development action that can provide the implementation of the maritime silk road programs through Interdependence and Interconnection, Regional Cooperation, Connectivity, Diplomatic Strategy of Openness and Inclusiveness, and Great Vision of Statemen. This will unify the paradigm shift development mechanisms and processes within change, innovation, idealism and freedom.

This is in consideration with Vision and Actions on Jointly Building Silk Road Economic Belt and 21st-Century Maritime Silk Road issued by the National Development and Reform Commission, Ministry of Foreign Affairs, and Ministry of Commerce of the People's Republic of China, with State Council authorization (March 2015). Likewise, it is reflective in the Belt and Road Initiative is in line with the purposes and principles of the UN Charter. It upholds the Five Principles of Peaceful Coexistence: mutual respect for each other's sovereignty and territorial integrity, mutual non-aggression, mutual non-interference in each other's internal affairs, equality and mutual benefit, and peaceful coexistence.

The Initiative is open for cooperation. It covers, but is not limited to, the area of the ancient Silk Road. It is open to all countries, and international and regional organizations for engagement, so that the results of the concerted efforts will benefit wider areas.

The Initiative is harmonious and inclusive. It advocates tolerance among civilizations, respects the paths and modes of development chosen by different countries, and supports dialogues among different civilizations on the principles of seeking common ground while shelving differences and drawing on each other's strengths, so that all countries can coexist in peace for common prosperity.

The Initiative follows market operation. It will abide by market rules and international norms, give play to the decisive role of the market in resource allocation and the primary role of enterprises, and let the governments perform their due functions.

The Initiative seeks mutual benefit. It accommodates the interests and concerns of all parties involved, and seeks a conjunction of interests and the "biggest common denominator" for cooperation so as to give full play to the wisdom and creativity, strengths and potentials of all parties.

The academic theoretical models include the following that must capture the essence of the underlying political and economic philosophy of the "Belt and Road Initiative" in the Asian region.

1. **Interdependence and Interconnection.** This represents the win-win cooperation of the Asian countries to undertake economic activities on common development that best suited to human and non-human undertakings in the specific areas of understanding in the geographical maritime activities in the contemporary time. This generates the interdependence of economic change through the transfer of technologies that are needed to further boost the production of goods and services in the area. This represents the utilization of the interdependence of social systems to achieve the quality programs in social, political and economic dimensions for world peace and development.

2. **Regional Cooperation.** This is a new type of international relations that provides the diplomatic support on mutual respect, consensus-building and accommodation which represents the peaceful co-existence of the Asian countries. The manifestation of idealism expounds in the improvement of quality of life as a result of the increasing employment and economic activities among the Asian countries. The peaceful co-existence is defined by mutual respect to be transparent on the economic interest that can be accommodated to sustain the flow of investments in the area. The provision of regional investments will ensure the collective accommodation with consensus-building measures for the economic development of the state.

3. **Connectivity and Economic Growth.** The underlying principles of the economic stimulus through the support of technological change through the strategic alliance in the investments for the maritime silk road. This can be successfully done by the support inclusive growth and technology transfer for the developing countries of Asia to pursue the much-needed economic investments in the area. The technological production of the economic enterprises and the utilization of the information technology brings a better interconnectivity and inter-regional cooperation initiative in the Asian region. It is the most important variable in the paradigm shift analysis of world peace and development.

4. **Diplomatic Strategy of Openness and Inclusiveness.** This future success of "Belt and Road Initiative" represents the openness and inclusiveness where there must be trust and appreciation through varied economic and political activities that would benefit the whole Asian region. The essence of idealism and freedom from the mature economic system is the peaceful cooperation to involve the countries to support regional cooperation to solve international issues such as international financial crisis, devastating disasters, and international historical disputes. The grant-in aid has to be designed to translate government services to employment generation, poverty alleviation and livelihood development program.

The development advocacy of "Belt and Road Initiative" must reflect the great vision of a leader or statemen for the Asian nations to form the regional alliance that will have the features of regional cooperation, connectivity with the strategy of openness and inclusiveness. The great vision embraces the development efforts of a leader within the equal sovereign rights and privileges to work for common good and general welfare to achieve the quality of life that the Asian people have been aspiring for in the centuries of economic struggles.

Furthermore, the maritime silk road in the Asian region reconnects each other by the development mechanism of change in the end view that interdependence and interconnection not simply on bilateral or multi-lateral agreement being forged to provide closer political and economic interest of the Asian nations. The win-win cooperation is designed to establish the technological development and exchange of knowledge and human resources to bring closer for the interconnection of the participating Asian countries.

Paradigm Shift of Economic Change of the One Belt One Road

The economic change deals with the first stage of initiative as to the regional structure of oneness, openness and inclusivity as the main feature of "Belt and Road Initiative." These are the important economic variables representing the initiative on multipolarization, globalization, cultural diversity, and non-traditional security mechanism:

1. *The international situation continues to experience profound and complex changes, with significant development in multipolarization and economic globalization.* The paradigm shift in "Belt and Road Initiative" discusses the strategic opportunity to complement the mulitpolarization and economic globalization. The Asian countries have the human resource capacity to adjust and support the capital intensive industry through utilization of the IT program. The political consideration as to the economic adoption of this program is designed to implement regional cooperation through openness and inclusiveness in order to identify the strengths and capabilities of the Asian countries. Likewise, economic globalization has been the emerging trend through borderless society that will bring nations of the world closer to each other.

2. *Cultural diversity and IT application are making constant progress while readjustment is accelerating in international landscape and order.* The economic change and innovation as the main mechanism for the paradigm shift of world peace and development is considering the current strategic strength of the IT integration in doing business for economic globalization. The closeness and understanding of the Asian countries have been articulated by the cultural diversity in the essence of oneness, inclusiveness and openness. This had been the reason for the revival of the maritime silk road that brought the closeness of the Asian neighbors in conformance with the regional cooperation, interdependence and openness that had been sustained in centuries of the economic development. This initiative is not limited to IT application and economic development but the cultural diversity program which is directed in the Confucius Classrooms and Institute.

3. *Countries around the world are losing no time in adjusting their development strategies, pursuing transformation and innovation, changing their economic development models, improving economic structures and opening up new horizons for further development.* The paradigm shift model for the "Belt and Road Initiative" has been recently recognized that the

economic development models are the presence of technological and scientific integration and IT integration in the corporate promotion of investment in a given Asian country. The wide range of economic choices, continuing investment and marketing promotion program with widely accepted product lines will provide the economic development of the area.

4. *The world economy is still in a period of profound adjustment, with risks of low growth, low inflation and low demand interwoven with risks of high unemployment, high debt and high level of bubbles.* The performance and policies of major economies continue to diverge, and uncertainties in the economic climate remain prominent. The "Belt and Road Initiative" identifies the investment and livelihood support to withstand uncertainties brought about by the economic crisis which led to unemployment, rising cost of living and the increasing level of the poverty threshold line. It is expected that the regional cooperation will boost the economic activities in the entire geographical line of the maritime silk. The technological innovation and transfer of technical knowledge will gradually effect economic change in a given market. This provides the necessary economic and investment support to enhance employment, reduce poverty, increase the GDP and GNP.

5. *Geopolitical factors such as non-traditional security threats and global challenges are more at play and local turmoil keep cropping up.* The paradigm shift for peace and development requires the high degree of economic innovation and freedom to combat non-traditional security threats. This will be done through the forging bilateral or multi-lateral commitment to prevent the political and economic impact in the Asian countries. There are significant investment mechanisms for safety nets in the global challenges which the paradigm shift for regional collaboration and accommodation in providing balance of the global challenges. The "Belt and Road Initiative" has the development support mechanism underlying the implementation of energy and food security through the investment of infrastructure that will sustain the energy needs and increase the volume of agricultural products. The infrastructure requires funding assistance that "Belt and Road Initiative" will provide the necessary economic support in this area.

What is significant in the advocacy of "Belt and Road Initiative" advocated by President Xi Jinping is the strategic development of the Asian countries to bring the idea of closeness, oneness, and openness as part of the living tradition in the existence of the maritime silk road for many centuries. The revival of the regional cooperation and accommodation will bring closer diplomatic ties among the Asian countries which is the end product of the noble cause of peace and development which has not been fully achieved in the region. The past economic trades had been able to bring the dynamic interaction among the Asian traders because of the maritime silk road then the duplication of this economic and cultural experiences will promote the best interest for all mankind.

Development Visions and Strategic Opportunities of "One Belt One Road"

The noble cause for the quest of peace and development can be achieved through the following identified development visions of the "Belt and Road Initiative" as defined by President Xin Jinping :

1. To build a community of common destiny, we need to make sure that all countries respect one another and treat each other as equal.

2. To build a community of common destiny, we need to seek win-win cooperation and common development.

3. To build a community of common destiny, we need to pursue common, comprehensive, cooperative and sustainable security.

The unique development vision of "Belt and Road Initiative" is designed to bring global peace and development through a common destiny to embrace interdependence and recognition of sovereign state, regional cooperation and sustainable security to support the economic and political ties among the countries in the world. The role of China being a big country shoulders greater responsibilities for regional and world peace which is the foremost development vision of the " Belt and Road Initiative" that initiates equal rights for the international community in all regional and global affairs. The leadership of China ensures the international cooperation and accommodation for the countries around the world to participate "Belt and Road Initiative" that give strategic opportunity to implement the peace and development mechanisms on change, innovation, idealism and freedom.

This will be done by the Chinese government through the strategic implementation of the economic change that provides the support of infrastructure and investment which is further articulated by the presence of the economic resources for the participating countries to innovate through the technological development which will increase the investment and infrastructure development within a given regional area. The idealism will then achieve as the economic prosperity redounds to the after effect of quality of life for all. The development of inner character will be the result of the idealism by embracing development of self-esteem, freedom and deployment security to prevent the social exploitation among them. The highest level of freedom does not mean only on movement and action but the equal structure of the beneficial effects for all mankind to appreciate and recognize to attain the government vision of quality of life. The idea of freedom requires the citizens around the world to enjoy and economic resources for meaningful employment and prestige not on the hidden social exploitation where the rich controls the masses. The genuine freedom will be given to all people free from exploring the world by bringing peace in the family no longer experience hunger and manipulation of social classes including the reduction of social problems.

On the other hand, the development vision of the win-win cooperation considers the multi-facet dimension of engagement not only economic activities but also political, security, cultural and other fields. The macro-economic policies in the win-win cooperation are the diplomatic engagements to the idea of openness and inclusiveness embodied in mutual respect and recognition which serve as the focal point of development in the areas of infrastructure development, employment generation, enterprise development and cultural exchange program. It must be directed to the multi-lateral cooperation through the regional clustering of the maritime silk road areas that will move closer to the One Common System of Economic and Cultural Development based on the principles of "Road and Belt Initiative."

These are needed development reforms for the international macro-policies through the promotion of global economic governance and upholding an open world economy. The spill-over effects of openness and inclusiveness provide the enhancement of economic governance that will support the development of regional industries, technological hubs, export processing centers, and regional manufacturing complementation. The oneness approach will bring all the economic resources based on the interdependence of strategic strength that can be accommodated to all nations.

The ASEAN (Plus One) integration plays an important role through the China-ASEAN community can articulate the economic and financial resources to participate in the "Belt and Road Initiative" in the areas of cultural diversity, academic exchange, infrastructure assistance, economic integration hub and other strategic activities . Specifically, the economic integration has resulted to one system of economic development for all ASEAN countries that will move closer to open regionalism through exchanges and cooperation with China under the roof of " Belt and Road Initiative."

The initiative of President Xi Jinping advocated that *China proposes that plans be formulated regarding connectivity building in East Asia and Asia at large to advance full integration in infrastructure, policies and institutions and personnel flow. We may increase maritime connectivity, speed up institution building for marine cooperation in Asia, and step up cooperation in marine economy, environmental protection, disaster management and fishery. This way, we could turn the seas of Asia into seas of peace, friendship and cooperation for Asian countries.*

The ASEAN Integration plus One (China) brings the economic regional complementation of varied development activities through maritime connectivity that will speed up cooperation on the seas of Asia for peace, friendship and cooperation for Asian countries along the following :

1. **Maritime Economy.** The longs standing maritime disputes may hold the key to peaceful development of the ASEAN region through " Belt and Road Initiative" to reminisce and support the old Maritime Silk Road for the multi-lateral participation in regional maritime economic collaboration.

2. **Environmental Protection.** The maritime silk road inter-agency monitoring on environmental protection with the integration of sustainable development for this program.

3. **Disaster Management.** The "Belt and Road Initiative" embodies the oneness of regional cooperation to provide a helping hand in the disaster mitigation and preparedness in all Asian region to support those who are victims of natural and man-made calamities.

4. **Fishery.** The regional cooperation through multi-lateral agreement must be forged through the leadership of China in the development and implementation of "Belt and Road Initiative" Fishery Program that will benefit the entire fishermen of Asia. The regional fishery hub has been well in placed in the maritime

silk road for centuries of peaceful development in the fishery resource generation.

These are important development activities of "Belt and Road Initiative" to erase all doubts as attributed by any forms of mistrust which sometimes incomprehensible to human imagination. The paradigm shift of peace and development in "Belt and Road Initiative" repeatedly discussing the ideals of oneness, openness and inclusivity within the framework of mutual trust and respect of the international community. This is designed for world peace that will start in the ASEAN region which will be later on spill over to the other Asian countries. It had been successful in the past centuries of the development of maritime silk road then it can be duplicated for the young generation to appreciate the oneness and openness of mankind. The values and spirits of time are too much engrossed on distrust and solving conflict. These are rehabilitative mechanisms that destroy nations around the world. The peaceful settlement of political conflicts relies so much on trust and respect. We can only do lasting world peace when the young generation embrace the lasting image of regional cooperation, respect and trust among all mankind.

The philosophical idea of Mencius presented by President Xi Jinping embraces real change in the heart and mind of the Asian race from the main thought of exchange and dialogue. *Mencius, the great philosopher in ancient China, said, "Things are born to be different. "Civilizations are only unique, and no one is superior to the other. There need to be more exchange and dialogue among civilizations and development models, so that each could draw on the strength of the other and all could thrive and prosper by way of mutual learning and common development. Let us promote inter-civilization exchanges to build bridges of friendship for our people, drive human development and safeguard peace of the world.*

Our great ancestors who had been living the mutual exchanges and dialogues in their quest of maritime trade in the Asian region. Yet no one appeared to be the adversary of the inter-civilization exchanges in the east. They had the peace of heart and dedication to be in dialogue with our friendly neighbors in the east. These were the true path of peaceful development that attributed by the change, innovation, idealism and freedom. We have done that before that we can also do it now for sake of the young generation to follow the same path in the maritime silk road that we now embrace " Road and Belt Initiative."

Great Nation and Statesmen Embracing "Road and Belt Initiative" through Maritime Silk Road Confucius Institute

The Asian nations have been living in harmony with the great civilization of the past that can again unify the revival of the maritime silk road where great Chinese leaders and statesmen as well can share our ancestor with products and culture throughout the world. The great Chinese leaders in the quest of the maritime silk road connected with them the compassion one Asian race revered so much respect and recognition of the neighboring countries of Asia. These were the ideals of peace and development that revolved around mutual respect and recognition that finally sustained the ideals of change, innovation, idealism and freedom.

The great leaders and statemen of China through the leadership of President Xi Jinping have finally offer the ideals of change, innovation, idealism and freedom through " Belt and Road Initiative" that will benefit the Asian and all countries of the world. Furthermore, China stands at the apex of leading those countries participating in the "Belt and Road Initiative:" These are the justifications of President Xi Jinping in realizing the great national rejuvenation to embrace diplomatic cooperation in the duplicating the maritime silk road which had been successful in the ideals of oneness, openness and inclusivity in "Road and Belt Initiative."

Under the leadership of China in initiating "Road and Belt Initiative" will provide necessary economic assistance and support to identify geographical areas that are feasible in the maritime silk road areas that will embrace the ideal of change and innovation.

> *The Chinese economy has entered a state of new normal. It is shifting gear from high speed to medium-to-high speed growth, from an extensive model that emphasized scale and speed to a more intensive one emphasizing quality and efficiency, and from being driven by investment in production factors to being driven by innovation.*

Accordingly, President Xi Jinping mentioned the active role of China in the investment and economic production and social development (a) Continue to be responsive to the new trends and take initiatives to shape the new normal in our favor; (b) Improve quality and efficiency, and give even greater priority to shifting the growth model and adjusting the structure of development; (c) Make more solid efforts to boost economic development and deepen reforms and opening-up; (d) Take more initiatives to unleash the creativity and ingenuity of the people, be more effective in safeguarding equity and social justice, raise people's living standards.

Furthermore, the Chinese regional cooperation and partnerships with the Asian countries will continue to bring more opportunities of trade, growth, and investment. This may mean to apply the advocacy of the paradigm shift of world peace as mentioned by President Xi Jinping that

"China needs most is a harmonious and stable domestic environment and a peaceful and tranquil. What is important interesting international environment. Turbulence or war runs against the fundamental interests of the Chinese people. The Chinese nation loves peace and has, since ancient times, held high such philosophies that "harmony is the most valuable", "peace and harmony should prevail" and "all men under heaven are brothers".

"... China will be steadfast in pursuing the independent foreign policy of peace, the path of peaceful development, the win-win strategy of opening-up, and the approach of upholding justice while pursuing shared interests. China will work to promote a new type of international relations of win-win cooperation and will always remain a staunch force for world peace and common development."

The Chinese President initiative provides the Paradigm Shift of World Peace and Development with the special heart and spirit in building friendship and partnership in the Asian countries. This had been experienced in the past centuries that China as the seat of ancient civilization extended the diplomatic support as far as the middle east to empower the ancient sovereign state to form trade alliances particularly in the Asian countries that respected and recognized the political and economic system during that time.

Close neighbors are better than distant relatives. This is a simple truth that the Chinese people got to know in ancient times. That explains China's firm commitment to building friendship and partnership with its neighbors to foster an amicable, secure and prosperous neighborhood.

Under the principle of amity, sincerity, mutual benefit and inclusiveness, China is working actively to deepen win-win cooperation and connectivity with its neighbors to bring them even more benefit with its own development. China has signed treaties of good-neighborliness, friendship and cooperation with eight of its neighbors and is holding discussion to sign a same treaty with ASEAN. China stands ready to sigh such a treaty with all its neighbors to provide strong support for the development of bilateral relations as well as prosperity and stability in the region.

The significant implementation of this "Belt and Road Initiative" is the diplomatic engagement of the participating countries in the world to be a part in shaping the regional cooperation in the economic activities of the maritime silk road. President Xi Jinping mentioned:

"In promoting this initiative, China will follow the principle of wide consultation, joint contribution and shared benefits. The programs of development will be open and inclusive, not exclusive. They will be a real chorus comprising all countries along the routes, not a solo for China itself. To develop the Belt and Road is not to replace existing mechanisms or initiatives for regional cooperation. Much to the contrary, we will build on the existing basis to help countries align their development strategies and form complementarity. Currently, more than 60 countries along the routes and international organizations have shown interest in taking part in the development of the Belt and the Road. The "Belt and Road" and the AIIB are both open initiatives. We welcome all countries along the routes and in Asia, as well as our friends and partners around the world, to take an active part in these endeavors.

Chapter X
Vision and Actions on Jointly Building Silk Road Economic Belt and 21st-Century Maritime Silk Road

This chapter was published in the first book of Confucius Institute of Maritime Silk Road: A Diplomatic Strategy of World Peace and Development (2015) which provides the information about the Vision and Actions on Jointly Silk Road Economic Belt and 21st Century Maritime Silk Road issued by the National Development and Reform Commission, Ministry of Foreign Affairs, and Ministry of Commerce of the People's Republic of China, with State Council authorization last March 2015 (First Edition 2015). It expounds the relevance of the educational and cultural exchange programs that can be adopted in the Maritime Silk Road Confucius Institute to promote World Peace and Development. The diplomatic cooperation in the continental regions of Asia, Europe , Africa including America brings closer ties for educational and cultural exchanges that relates to the Confucian Philosophy and Chinese language, culture and history. Furthermore, the Maritime Silk Road Confucius Institute discusses important educational and cultural model as experienced by the Romchatra Foundation in sustaining the First Confucius Classroom and Traimit Model in Thailand to its co-existence in the implementation of the ASEAN integration.

A. Historical Perspectives of the Marine Silk Road

The historical account of the Marine Silk Road describes the diplomatic peace and unity among the major civilizations of Asia, Europe and Africa that had been experienced for thousands of years. It symbolizes the closeness of human hearts and spirits to bring world peace even in the 21st century. There has been mutual respect and understanding of the different countries around the world in the exploration and opening of the trade that resulted to the cultural exchanges.

More than two millennia ;;ago the diligent and courageous people of Eurasia explored and opened up several routes of trade and cultural exchanges that linked the major civilizations of Asia, Europe and Africa, collectively called the Silk Road by later generations. For thousands of years, the Silk Road Spirit – "peace and cooperation, openness and inclusiveness, mutual learning and mutual benefit" – has been passed from generation to generation, promoted the progress of human civilization, and contributed greatly to the prosperity and development of the countries along the Silk Road. Symbolizing communication and cooperation between the East and the West, the Silk

Road Spirit is a historic and cultural heritage shared by all countries around the world.

Director General Li Yong of the United Nations Industrial Development Organization (UNIDO) in his Welcome Remarks of the Promotion Week of the Economic Belt along the Silk Road last October 6, 2014 at Vienna International Center organized by the Department of Culture of Shanxi Province expounded his view admiring the ancestors creation of mutual prosperity and progress in the true meaning of the silk road :

> *Two thousand years ago, Zhang Qian, a famous Chinese diplomat in the Han Dynasty, was first sent as an envoy to the Central Asian countries and opened up the fabled Silk Road connecting Europe and Asia from east to west. Today, we have the chance to recall the prosperity along the Silk Road, and to gain an impression of how the merchants travelled and conducted business along that ancient trade route. This event of today gives us all a better understanding of the true meaning and spirit of the Silk Road, and bears testimony to the deep rooted and far reaching efforts of our ancestors to connect with other people and nations in order to create mutual prosperity. I cannot stop admiring the endeavor of our ancestors in pursuit of a better life, which should serve as an example for our generation as we seek to achieve development and progress through increased production and trade.*

In contemporary time, the idea of diplomatic initiative defines the inter-regional cooperation of all segments of the society to bring world peace and prosperity based from the Silk Road Spirit that provides closeness of the people in Asia, Africa and Europe for many centuries.

> *In the 21st century, a new era marked by the theme of peace, development, cooperation and mutual benefit, it is all the more important for us to carry on the Silk Road Spirit in face of the weak recovery of the global economy, and complex international and regional situations.*

The relevance of the Silk Road Economic Belt revives with the original initiative of the Chinese government through President XI Jinping when he visited Central Asia and Southeast Asia last September and October 2013. At the same year, Chinese Premier Li Keqiang in China-ASEAN Expo emphasized the need to build the Maritime Silk Road oriented towards ASEAN, and to create strategic propellers for hinterland development.

Accelerating the building of the Belt and Road can help promote the economic prosperity of the countries along the Belt and Road and regional economic cooperation, strengthen exchanges and mutual learning between different civilizations, and promote world peace and development. It is a great undertaking that will benefit people around the world.

The historical perspective of the Maritime Silk Road is an excellent diplomat idea to transform the peaceful co-existence of the Chinese descent around the world. It is now an effective instrument to share the complementation of world civilization within the presence of the silk road in Asia, Africa and Europe. As a diplomatic approach to provide world peace and development initiative by the Chinese government, it is morally right to bring closer the heart and soul of China that is deeply rooted from its historical tradition from economic trade to the cultural and educational divergence of the human society around the world.

In its application to the Maritime Silk Road Confucius Institute, it also provides support the exchanges and mutual learning between different civilizations :

1. **The cultural assimilation as the Chinese descent permanently residing in other ASEAN countries including Asia, Africa and Europe.** This represents the Chinese society in the world as ambassador of goodwill with the result of the intermarriage with other countries of the Economic Silk Road in the past.

2. **The complementation of the cultural and educational thought of the Chinese descent.** The cultural assimilation as a result of the inter-marriage responded to a unique cultural and educational thought throughout Asia, Africa and Europe. The strategic opportunity to appreciate the economic and cultural contributions in the development of Chinese culture and language around the world.

3. **The economic and cultural exchanges of Chinatown with economic cooperation from the Chinese government.** The important economic contribution of China around the world is the distinct recognition of Chinatown as the center of Chinese activities. The Chinese Chamber of Commerce contributed so much to the national economy of other countries around the world.

4. **The continuing cultural and educational advocacy of the Confucius Classrooms/Institutes.** This is a good opportunity for the Maritime Silk Road Confucius Institute to conduct cultural and historical research to be

disseminated in the international conferences and lectures. The establishments of the Chinese Classrooms/Institutes are sustained to provide training in Chinese language, culture and history that may still be adopted in the Maritime Silk Road Confucius Institute. It is the primary activities that can be done for the human society to be aware of the contribution of China around the world.

5. **The establishment of economic partnerships with the ASEAN region with the theme Maritime Silk Road Economic on Equal Collaboration**. This is an equal development opportunity to share the wealth and human resources of China and ASEAN countries in the development of China Sea in the Maritime Silk Road that produced economic prosperity of hundreds of years ago. The historical antecedents produced a remarkable diplomatic peace and development including the cultural assimilation of the Chinese descents who helped the ASEAN countries sustained the economic and cultural development if Chinatown and active participation of the Chinese Chamber of Commerce.

The cultural assimilation is the important contribution of the Chinese descent mingling with the genetic development of human society. The aforementioned cultural, educational and economic exchanges support of the Confucius Classrooms/ Institutes ensured its applicability as to the vision and mission the 21st Century Maritime Silk Road :

> *The Belt and Road Initiative is a systematic project, which should be jointly built through consultation to meet the interests of all, and efforts should be made to integrate the development strategies of the countries along the Belt and Road. The Chinese government has drafted and published the Vision and Actions on Jointly Building Silk Road Economic Belt and 21st-Century Maritime Silk Road to promote the implementation of the Initiative, instill vigor and vitality into the ancient Silk Road, connect Asian, European and African countries more closely and promote mutually beneficial cooperation to a new high and in new forms.* (Preface)

Although one of the major concerns of the "Belt and Road Initiative" is to address the international financial crisis, the China's initiative to embrace for global development that also brings world peace as the by-product of the educational and cultural exchange program of the human society.

As presented in the background of the Vision and Mission of the 21st Maritime Silk Road discusses the following development of China's support under "Belt and Road Initiative."

The initiative to jointly build the Belt and Road, embracing the trend towards a multipolar world, economic globalization, cultural diversity and greater IT application, is designed to uphold the global free trade regime and the open world economy in the spirit of open regional cooperation. It is aimed at promoting orderly and free flow of economic factors, highly efficient allocation of resources and deep integration of markets; encouraging the countries along the Belt and Road to achieve economic policy coordination and carry out broader and more in-depth regional cooperation of higher standards; and jointly creating an open, inclusive and balanced regional economic cooperation architecture that benefits all. Jointly building the Belt and Road is in the interests of the world community. Reflecting the common ideals and pursuit of human societies, it is a positive endeavor to seek new models of international cooperation and global governance, and will inject new positive energy into world peace and development.

The Belt and Road Initiative aims to promote the connectivity of Asian, European and African continents and their adjacent seas, establish and strengthen partnerships among the countries along the Belt and Road, set up all-dimensional, multi-tiered and composite connectivity networks, and realize diversified, independent, balanced and sustainable development in these countries. The connectivity projects of the Initiative will help align and coordinate the development strategies of the countries along the Belt and Road, tap market potential in this region, promote investment and consumption, create demands and job opportunities, enhance people-to-people and cultural exchanges, and mutual learning among the peoples of the relevant countries, and enable them to understand, trust and respect each other and live in harmony, peace and prosperity.

China's economy is closely connected with the world economy. China will stay committed to the basic policy of opening-up, build a new pattern of all-round opening-up, and integrate itself deeper into the world economic system. The Initiative will enable China to further expand and deepen its opening-up, and to strengthen its mutually beneficial cooperation with countries in Asia, Europe and Africa and the rest of the world. China is committed to shouldering more responsibilities and obligations within its capabilities, and making greater contributions to the peace and development of mankind.

In the attainment of World Peace, the Maritime Silk Road Confucius Institute adheres the diplomatic strategy through international cooperation and global governance in the implementation of the cultural and educational exchange program in the different field of specializations. In the case of the

Multipolar World, the advocacy of world peace carries the understanding of educational and cultural exchange ties even in the multiple center of power and influence to the different parts of the continent. The economic diplomacy provides deeper understanding and sharing of wealth and human resources about the Role of the Marine Silk Road for the global prosperity of the region. Furthermore, the ideals positive energy in pursuing world peace in the 21st Maritime Silk Road reflects on the global free trade, economic globalization, cultural diversity, greater IT application.

The Global Free Trade that has been well-established since the beginning of the silk road in Asia, Africa and Europe. In the 21st century, the global free trade defines in the spirit of open world economy in the spirit of regional cooperation. There are unique super-structure of educational , cultural, and economic system that may apply to the multi-layered bonding of the multipolar world with one purpose of creating world peace The open world economy replicates the Maritime Silk Road of the past that the convergence of the human development provides the greater level of social accessibility in commerce and industry.

The Chinese Chamber of Commerce and the diplomatic chain of economic development of China should provide the necessary support to bring the Confucius Institute Philosophy in the adherence of world peace and the international cooperation based from the ideals of "One Belt and One Road" for the greater economic prosperity. The economic globalization and greater IT applications are still part of the whole package of the development of "Belt and Road Initiative" to respond the technological change in the 21st century. However, the most important infusion of the technological and economic development must respond to a quality of human resources to bring unified cultural effort of social change. As to the role of the Confucius Institute of Maritime Silk Road, it provides the educational and cultural support in the acculturation process of human development within the symbiotic perspectives in the presence of Chinese descents and Chinese economic activities in the areas of global interest.

B. Principles of the Belt and Road Initiative

The Vision and Actions on Jointly Silk Road Economic Belt and 21st Century Maritime Silk Road has five (5) principles of Peaceful Coexistence in the Belt and Road Initiative namely : (1) mutual respect for each other's sovereignty and territorial integrity; (2) mutual non-aggression; (4) mutual non-interference of each other's internal affairs; and (5) equality and mutual benefit, and peaceful coexistence.

In the Keynote Speech of Executive Vice Foreign Minister Zhang Yesui at the Luncheon of the Third World Peace Forum at Liaoning Hotel last June 21, 2014 (Source : Ministry of Foreign Affairs of the People's Republic of China) expounded his opinion about Peaceful Coexistence :

Since the introduction of reform and opening up, China's foreign policy has been stable and consistent. We are firmly committed to an independent foreign policy of peace. We are firmly committed to developing comprehensive and friendly cooperation with all countries on the basis of the Five Principles of Peaceful Coexistence. And we are firmly committed to upholding our sovereignty, security and development interests. We are determined, in line with China's fundamental interests and the trend of peace, development and win-win cooperation, to pursue a new path of peaceful development by a major country. That is to say, we strive to develop ourselves through securing a peaceful international environment and maintain and promote world peace through our own development. We want the world's opportunities to work for China and China's opportunities to work for the world, and amidst such sound and win-win interaction, pursue peaceful development.

The China's diplomatic strategy for peaceful coexistence has open up a new window of educational and cultural opportunities to achieve world peace. It is guided by a comprehensive and friendly cooperation with the fundamental interest to secure a peaceful international environment in order to achieve a win-win interaction of the human society in the world.

In the case of "Belt and Road Initiative," these are the core areas on principles of peaceful coexistence covered in the Silk Economic Belt and 21st Century Maritime Silk Road :

The Initiative is open for cooperation. It covers, but is not limited to, the area of the ancient Silk Road. It is open to all countries, and international and regional organizations for engagement, so that the results of the concerted efforts will benefit wider areas.

The Initiative is harmonious and inclusive. It advocates tolerance among civilizations, respects the paths and modes of development chosen by different countries, and supports dialogues among different civilizations on the principles of seeking common ground while shelving differences and drawing on each other's strengths, so that all countries can coexist in peace for common prosperity.

The Initiative follows market operation. It will abide by market rules and international norms, give play to the decisive role of the market in resource allocation and the primary role of enterprises, and let the governments perform their due functions.

The Initiative seeks mutual benefit. It accommodates the interests and concerns of all parties involved, and seeks a conjunction of interests and the "biggest common denominator" for cooperation so as to give full play to the wisdom and creativity, strengths and potentials of all parties.

As to its application in the Maritime Silk Road Confucius Institute, the principles of peaceful coexistence are the basic tenets to achieve world peace. The peaceful coexistence defines by standard diplomatic strategy through equality and mutual benefits by providing support on educational and cultural exchanges which is open to all countries but not limited to the ancient silk road.

The Maritime Silk Road Confucius Institute entails harmonious and inclusive support through dialogues among different civilizations. Primarily, it provides support on the educational and cultural exchanges in the field of Chinese language, culture, history and arts within the theme of the Maritime Silk Road. This gives more academic opportunity to explore the fusion of cultural diversity in the social acculturation and assimilation of the flourishing Chinese trade with diplomatic contacts in the different continents of the world. The educational and cultural exchanges may be done through academic training, cultural and historical research studies, lectures and international conferences to ensure the sharing of ideas and sentiments to achieve world peace and development.

C. Framework of the "Belt and Road Initiative"

The Chinese government with its diplomatic effort on the Belt and Road Initiative is a manifestation for win-win cooperation to reach out of the countries of the world. This is also a holistic diplomatic approach to fulfill peaceful coexistence of the Chinese government through the genuine Belt and Road Initiative. The advocacy of world peace is well in place in this development framework for the "Belt and Road Initiative :"

The Belt and Road Initiative is a way for win-win cooperation that promotes common development and prosperity and a road towards peace and friendship by enhancing mutual understanding and trust, and strengthening all-round exchanges. The Chinese government advocates peace and cooperation, openness and inclusiveness, mutual learning and mutual benefit. It promotes practical cooperation in all fields, and works to build a community of shared interests, destiny and responsibility featuring mutual political trust, economic integration and cultural inclusiveness.

The Confucius Institute of Maritime Silk Road has to adopt the development advocacy on the ideas of *peace and cooperation, openness and inclusiveness, mutual learning and mutual benefit. It promotes practical cooperation in all fields, and works to build a community of shared interests, destiny and responsibility featuring mutual political trust, economic integration and cultural inclusiveness.*

Based from the economic development framework under the Vision and Actions on Jointly Silk Road Economic Belt and 21st Century Maritime Silk Road, it primarily focuses the following continental and geographical areas :

(1) The Belt and Road run through the continents of Asia, Europe and Africa, connecting the vibrant East Asia economic circle at one end and developed European economic circle at the other, and encompassing countries with huge potential for economic development.

(2) The Silk Road Economic Belt focuses on bringing together China, Central Asia, Russia and Europe (the Baltic); linking China with the Persian Gulf and the Mediterranean Sea through Central Asia and West Asia; and connecting China with Southeast Asia, South Asia and the Indian Ocean.

(3) The 21st-Century Maritime Silk Road is designed to go from China's coast to Europe through the South China Sea and the Indian Ocean in one route, and from China's coast through the South China Sea to the South Pacific in the other.

As part of the diplomatic strategy that permeates in the global economy of the "Belt and Road Initiative," the Maritime Silk Road Confucius Institute has educational, social and cultural attributes deeply rooted from its designed to go from China's coast to Europe through the South China Sea and the Indian Ocean in one route, and from China's coast through the South China Sea to the South Pacific. The silk products (including Chinese porcelain jars) did not only bring the economic goods but the Chinese cultural life that spread throughout the coastal areas and trade centers that eventually amalgamated in the different cultures of the human society in the world. This brings world peace as Chinese government provides the diplomatic support including economic investments on infrastructure development to ensure the sustainability of the past generation effort in the economic activities in the Maritime Silk Road.

Furthermore, the current initiative of the Maritime Silk Road connects from the land and sea routes :

1) On land, the Initiative will focus on jointly building a new Eurasian Land Bridge and developing China-Mongolia-Russia, China-Central Asia-West Asia and China-Indochina Peninsula economic corridors by taking advantage of international transport routes, relying on core cities along the Belt and Road and using key economic industrial parks as cooperation platforms.

2) At sea, the Initiative will focus on jointly building smooth, secure and efficient transport routes connecting major sea ports along the Belt and Road. The China-Pakistan Economic Corridor and the Bangladesh-China-India-Myanmar Economic Corridor are closely related to the Belt and Road Initiative, and therefore require closer cooperation and greater progress.

These are strategic opportunities to widen the diplomatic collaboration and cooperation among sovereign states to revive the former glory of the silk road vested by common interest of economic prosperity and development for world peace. The Maritime Silk Road Confucius Institute has its common interest to educate and share the ideas as to the systemic approach of economic and cultural development that brings the window of opportunity as to the ambitious economic vision of the opening-up of and cooperation among the countries along the " Belt and Road Initiative :"

> *Countries should work in concert and move towards the objectives of mutual benefit and common security. To be specific, they need to improve the region's infrastructure, and put in place a secure and efficient network of land, sea and air passages, lifting their connectivity to a higher level; further enhance trade and investment facilitation, establish a network of free trade areas that meet high standards, maintain closer economic ties, and deepen political trust; enhance cultural exchanges; encourage different civilizations to learn from each other and flourish together; and promote mutual understanding, peace and friendship among people of all countries.*

D. Cooperation Priorities of Belt and Road Initiative

The cooperation priorities of the Vision and Actions on Jointly Silk Road Economic Belt and 21st Century Maritime Silk Road have mainly provided support to the economic investments and trade from the different continental regions of the world. The "Belt and Road Initiative" defines the diplomatic idea that *"Countries along the Belt and Road have their own resource advantages and their economies are mutually complementary. Therefore, there is a great potential and space for cooperation. They should promote policy coordination, facilities connectivity, unimpeded trade, financial integration and people-to-people bonds as their five major goals, and strengthen cooperation in the following key areas: (1) Policy Coordination ; (2) Facilities Connectivity; (3) Unimpeded trade; (4) Financial Integration; and (5) People to People bond."*

Interestingly, the Confucius Institute of Maritime has applied the cooperation priorities in support of the educational, cultural and social processes for the Vision and Actions on Jointly Silk Road Economic Belt and 21st Century Maritime Silk Road along People to People bond and support of cultural heritage :

People-to-people bond provides the public support for implementing the Initiative. We should carry forward the spirit of friendly cooperation of the Silk Road by promoting extensive cultural and academic exchanges, personnel exchanges and cooperation, media cooperation, youth and women exchanges and volunteer services, so as to win public support for deepening bilateral and multilateral cooperation.

We should send more students to each other's countries, and promote cooperation in jointly running schools. China provides 10,000 government scholarships to the countries along the Belt and Road every year. We should hold culture years, arts festivals, film festivals, TV weeks and book fairs in each other's countries; cooperate on the production and translation of fine films, radio and TV programs; and jointly apply for and protect World Cultural Heritage sites. We should also increase personnel exchange and cooperation between countries along the Belt and Road.

We should enhance cooperation in and expand the scale of tourism; hold tourism promotion weeks and publicity months in each other's countries; jointly create competitive international tourist routes and products with Silk Road features; and make it more convenient to apply for tourist visa in countries along the Belt and Road. We should push forward cooperation on the 21st-Century Maritime Silk Road cruise tourism program. We should carry out sports exchanges and support countries along the Belt and Road in their bid for hosting major international sports events.

We should strengthen cooperation with neighboring countries on epidemic information sharing, the exchange of prevention and treatment technologies and the training of medical professionals, and improve our capability to jointly address public health emergencies. We will provide medical assistance and emergency medical aid to relevant countries, and carry out practical cooperation in maternal and child health, disability rehabilitation, and major infectious diseases including AIDS, tuberculosis and malaria. We will also expand cooperation on traditional medicine.

We should increase our cooperation in science and technology, establish joint labs (or research centers), international technology transfer centers and maritime cooperation centers, promote sci-tech personnel exchanges, cooperate in tackling key sci-tech problems, and work together to improve sci-tech innovation capability.

We should integrate existing resources to expand and advance practical cooperation between countries along the Belt and Road on youth employment, entrepreneurship training, vocational skill development, social security management, public administration and management and in other areas of common interest.

We should give full play to the bridging role of communication between political parties and parliaments, and promote friendly exchanges between legislative bodies, major political parties and political organizations of countries along the Belt and Road. We should carry out exchanges and cooperation among cities, encourage major cities in these countries to become sister cities, focus on promoting practical cooperation, particularly cultural and people-to-people exchanges, and create more lively examples of cooperation. We welcome the think tanks in the countries along the Belt and Road to jointly conduct research and hold forums.

We should increase exchanges and cooperation between non-governmental organizations of countries along the Belt and Road, organize public interest activities concerning education, health care, poverty reduction, biodiversity and ecological protection for the benefit of the general public, and improve the production and living conditions of poverty-stricken areas along the Belt and Road. We should enhance international exchanges and cooperation on culture and media, and leverage the positive role of the Internet and new media tools to foster harmonious and friendly cultural environment and public opinion.

Based from the cooperation mechanisms and priorities of the "Belt and Road Initiative," the operations of the Maritime Silk Road Confucius Institute can adopt the promotion of extensive cultural and academic exchanges, personnel exchanges and cooperation, media cooperation, youth and women exchanges and volunteer service. These are the broad range of development programs to win public support for deepening bilateral and multilateral cooperation among the nations of the world. There are clear indications that the following cooperation mechanisms and priorities are part of the prospective development programs of the Marine Silk Road Confucius Institute.

These are the expanded programs of initiative to distinctly contribute to the implementation of the Confucius Institute of Maritime Silk Road :

1. The Maritime Silk Road Festivals that would include through the arts festivals, film festivals, TV weeks and book fairs in each other's countries; cooperate on the production and translation of fine films, radio and TV programs.

The Confucius Institutes adopt the academe-media linkages to identify the presence of the Maritime Silk Road of great importance that can exclusively open up new windows of opportunities to discover and share the knowledge about the Chinese people striving to provide economic and cultural contributions in the specific silk road activities in the past.

2. The Medical and Allied Health Cooperation in support of the Maritime Silk Road on the basis of the utilization of the Chinese Alternative Medicine.

The Confucius Institutes through the academe-public health linkages may respond the point of origin as to the alternative medicine in the Silk road. The cultural diversity provides the medical response as to the regional cooperation among nations to the presence of the alternative medicine in the maritime silk road. The Chinese medicine is now part of the 21st century revival of the traditional medicine which is called the alternative medicine that can be found from the different silk road routes in the past.

E. Science and Technology International Cooperation in the Continental Areas of the Maritime Silk Road

The Confucius Institutes spell out for the support of the educational and cultural exchange programs. However, the expanded development program for the Confucius Institute of Maritime Silk Road through the economic silk road provides the academe-science linkages to universities with Confucius Institutes in collaboration with other departments and divisions in science and technology to pursue the promotion of international research linkages through joint ventures on sci-tech innovation. The clustered structure in science and technology depends on the regional continental areas of the economic belt for the silk road.

4. The youth employment, entrepreneurship training, vocational skill development, social security management, public administration and management and in other areas of common interest.

The Chinese language and culture can still be part of the cultural training in the implementation of the aforementioned areas of common interests. The articulation of the employment development program integrates the manufacturing of Chinese products along utilization of the Chinese designs for paintings and sculptures with the inclusion of cultural tourism.

Furthermore, there are innovative ways for the creation of the Confucius Institute of Maritime Silk Road to carry out diplomatic exchanges including organization of public interest activities concerning education, health care, poverty reduction, biodiversity and ecological protection for the benefit of the general public, and improve the production and living conditions of poverty-stricken areas along the Belt and Road.

Chapter XI
Phraprommangkalachan's Initiative on "Belt and Road Initiative" through Maritime Silk Road Confucius Institute

The "Belt and Road Initiative" through the Confucius Institute of Maritime Silk Road provides the paradigm shift model for world peace and development for the educational, cultural and academic models to engage in the participation of the Asian nations. The first series of the book defines its roles of the Confucius Institute of Maritime Silk Road as a diplomatic strategy to attain World Peace and Development. This is the second part of the book that spells out the paradigm shift mechanisms in attaining world peace and development though change, innovation, idealism and freedom to clearly define the economic magnitude dealing with the infrastructure and investment support for those countries participating in "Belt and Road Initiative." However, this section expounds the non-tangible ideas through innovative ideas and practices to realign the principles of "Belt and Road Initiative" in openness and inclusiveness in the academic and cultural aspects of development for the Asian nations.

A. The Wisdom and Compassion for World Peace and Development

The Maritime Silk Road Confucius Institute was founded by Phraphrommankalachan to create a new way in the promotion of Chinese history, culture and language in the educational institutions, government offices, and private organizations which was established during the 40th anniversary of the diplomatic relations between China and Thailand. Phraprommangkalachan in his speech during the establishment of the First Confucius Institute of Marine Silk Road said that, Chinese President Xi Jinping's support of "Belt and Road Initiative" diplomatic strategy embodies a great contribution China makes to world peace and to the mutual development of neighboring countries.

In the report of Hanban (2015), the establishment of the Confucius Institute of Maritime Silk Road aims to better develop and advance the Chinese language education in Thailand as a pivot on the Maritime Silk Road and to facilitate exchanges between China and Thailand in all fields as it also marks the starting point of 2015 ASEAN Integration. At present, there are 14 Confucius Institutes and 18 Confucius Classrooms in Thailand, and the number of Chinese learners has exceeded 850,000.

B. The First "Confucius Institute of Maritime Silk Road" Established in Thailand [Source: Hanban 2015-07-06)

On the morning of June 24th, the "Confucius Institute of Maritime Silk Road" jointly applied by 27 educational institutions in Thailand was established and its inauguration ceremony was launched in Dhurakij Pundit University (DPU). Over 600 representatives from various circles attended the ceremony, including Madam Xu Lin, Chief Executive of Confucius Institute Headquarters and Director General of Hanban, Master Phraprommangkalachan, President of Romchatra Foundation, Thailand, Lieutenant General Surachet Chaiwong, Deputy Minister of the Ministry of Education in Thailand, Ning Fukui, Chinese Ambassador to Thailand, Varakorn Samakoses, President of Dhurakij Pundit University and Zhong Yinghua, Vice President of Tianjin Normal University.

At 10 A.M., the auditorium of Dhurakij Pundit University was already decorated with lights and festoons. Students from the Confucius Classroom at Traimit Wittayalai High School pounded on drums and gongs and performed Chinese lion dance, expressing the warmest welcome to the guests. Students from the Culture Center in Dhurakij Pundit University gave a traditional Thai blessing dance Nattasin, and those from the Confucius Classroom at Rayong Wittayakorm School performed a Chinese dance Thousand-Hand Avalokitesvara Bodhisattva. Later, President Varakorn, Ambassador Ning Fukui, Vice Minister Surachet, President Phraprommangkalachan and Madam Xu Lin delivered speeches respectively and then inaugurated the Confucius Institute of Maritime Silk

Road together.

Phraprommangkalachan said in his speech that, Chinese President Xi Jinping's support of "Belt and Road Initiative" as part of diplomatic strategy embodies a great contribution China makes to world peace and to the mutual development of neighboring countries. The year of 2015 marks the starting point of ASEAN Integration and also the 40th anniversary of the establishment of diplomatic relations between China and Thailand. The establishment of the Maritime Silk Road Confucius Institute aims to better develop and advance the Chinese language education in Thailand as a pivot on the Maritime Silk Road and to facilitate exchanges between China and Thailand in all fields.

C. Confucius Institute of Maritime Silk Road

The First Confucius Institute of Maritime Silk Road was founded by Phraphrommankalachan to create a new way in the promotion of Chinese history, culture and language in the educational institutions, government

offices, and private organizations which was established during the 40th anniversary of diplomatic relations between China and Thailand.

Phraprommangkalachan in his speech during the establishment of the First Confucius Institute of Marine Silk Road said that, Chinese President Xi Jinping's initiation of "One Belt and One Road" diplomatic strategy embodies a great contribution that China makes to world peace and to the mutual development of neighboring countries. In the report of Hanban (2015), the establishment of the Confucius Institute of Maritime Silk Road aims to better develop and advance the Chinese language education in Thailand as a pivot on the Maritime Silk Road and to facilitate exchanges between China and Thailand in all fields as it also marks the starting point of 2015 ASEAN Integration. At present, there are 14

Confucius Institutes and 18 Confucius Classrooms in Thailand, and the number of Chinese learners has exceeded 850,000.

Dedication of the Book on A Diplomatic Strategy for World Peace and Development

This book provides the ultimate development policy in "One Belt One Road" that transcribes from the various international conferences in the Maritime Silk Road in the Asian region. The inclusion of other chapters of this book gives the sustained program advocacy of the Confucius Institute for the worldwide awareness on the academic involvement of the Universities and Colleges to further study the "One Belt One Road" Initiative that the H.E. Chinese President Xi Jinping particularly in the development theme on Change, Innovation, Idealism and Freedom.

The substantial ideas of this book entitled "Confucius Institute of Maritime Silk Road: A Diplomatic Strategy of World Peace and Development" has supported this development theme of the "One Belt One Road" Initiative:

I dedicate this book to the people who opted to live
in harmony with the genuine hearts of mankind to restore peace
and development of nations in the world . As it transcends from the former grandeur of
the maritime silk road of the Chinese merchants and traders that connected the heart and
soul of the human society bounded by distinct beliefs and traditions in the continental
regions of Asia, Africa and Europe.

This contributed to the metamorphosis of a new form
of cultural and social life that assimilated and amalgamated the human society of Asia
which transported across Europe and Africa including America unconsciously working
together for the common economic goal in the contemporary time.

I also dedicate the Chinese and Thai people of the generosity
to work together to bring peace and development of the Asian region in the
implementation of the Confucius Institutes. Their priceless educational and cultural efforts
to bring the Chinese language and culture closer to their hearts and minds to achieve the
nirvana of life.

The love, respect and generosity of human society always
dictated by the diplomatic strategy mediated by the willingness of nations to trust each
other for the sake of peace and development of the future of our children. Finally, the
enlightened spirits always defined by the world leaders on the interests of nations to bring
peaceful coexistence as a genuine way to express the collective actions of the human

society...

D. Traimit Educational Model for the First Confucius School in Thailand

Traimitwittayalai Public High School is exclusively for boys located in the Traimit Temple compound which offers lessons to students from junior high to senior high school. In 2000, TWHS was named by the Ministry of Education as the "Chinese Language and Culture Center of Bangkok" and was later recognized as the "Center for the Promotion of Quality-Oriented Education in Chinese in the Chinese Language and Culture of Bangkok "by the Basic Education Division of Thailand.

In early 2000, Traimitwittayalai High School started to teach Chinese, and signed a Sister School Agreement with Tianjin Experimental High School two (2) years later. In 2006, with the approval of Hanban, it established Confucius Classroom at Traimitwittayalai High School. This was the first Confucius classroom in the world. It was founded in order to teach the Chinese language and spread Chinese culture for overseas students.

The Confucius Classroom at Traimitwittayalai offers the following Chinese teaching courses and programs according to the local instance: (1) Teach Chinese and sponsor cultural activities and Chinese competitions; (2) Train teachers to teach Chinese in primary and middle schools; (3) Organize summer and winter camp in China for primary and middle school students; and (4) Compile teaching materials.

The Chinese government has the obligation of the Hanban Headquarters: (1) to authorize the use of the title "Confucius Classroom", and provide logos and classroom emblems; (2) to provide the necessary start-up fund, and provide a set amount of annual fund according to needs; (3) to provide 1,000 volumes of books, audio-visual, multimedia materials and courseware, and authorize the use of online courses; and (4) to send Chinese instructors or volunteers according to needs and pay for their air fares and salaries.

The obligations of Confucius Classroom at Traimitwittayalai: (1) to provide an appropriate site for the Confucius Classroom to carry out its activities; to provide the necessary conditions and facility management to establish the Confucius Classroom and take charge of the setting, management, and maintenance; (2) to provide necessary administrative personnel (full time or part-time) the related payment and open the special account for the Confucius Classroom in the local Bank of China; (3) to provide necessary working conditions for the Chinese instructors; (4) assist the Chinese party in the classroom with all immigration procedures; and (5) agree to discuss with the headquarters any further requirements of the Confucius Classroom.

However, the main focus of educational cooperation and the one that has had the most impact on Thailand is Chinese language teaching. Since 1992 when the teaching of Chinese language in public and private educational institutions was officially permitted by the Thai government after about half a century of tight control, there has been an unprecedented demand for Chinese language teachers in the country. In response to this situation, an agreement was reached for China to send volunteer Chinese language teachers to Thailand, among other steps taken, which started in 2003 with the initial batch of 23 people, an unprecedented measure taken by the Chinese government to help overseas Chinese language teaching through voluntary teachers. By 2009 the number of volunteer teachers sent to Thailand increased to 1,000 a year, and further increased to around 1200 since 2010, and by this year 11 batches with a total of around 7,000 voluntary teachers have been sent to Thailand making Thailand the largest volunteer teacher recipients' country across the globe.

In 2005, one year after China established the first Confucius institute in South Korea, a proposal of establishing a Confucius Institute in Thailand was brought up, and the first agreement was signed in Beijing between China's Hanban (Office of Chinese Language Council International) and Thailand's Kasetsart University to set up the first Confucius Institute, initially named Confucius Institute in Bangkok. By the end of 2006, based on the agreement between Thai Ministry of Education and China's Hanban, 10 out of the 12 Confucius institutes and one (1) Confucius classroom, the first in the world, were officially opened.

On November 18, 2006, Pang Li then was the First Secretary of the Education Section of Chinese Embassy in Thailand and Kwan Ying General Secretary of Thai Minister of the Ministry of Education attended the unveiling ceremony of the world's first Confucius Classroom at Traimitwittayalai High School. Under the leadership of Hanban, Confucius Classroom at Traimitwittayalai High School launched many activities on education and cultural exchanges between China and Thailand by the efforts made by the Chinese and Thai partners, especially the support provided by Venerable Phradhamphawanawitkron. As first Confucius Classroom, her Majesty Queen of Thailand Maha Vajiralongkorn, Her Royal Highness Princess of Thailand Sirindhorn, her Royal Highness Princess of Thailand Chula horn Walalak and over 30 Chinese and Thai political leaders and military senior officials participated in the activities held in Confucius Classroom at Traimittwittayalai High School.

In 2010, the Thai Confucius Classroom through the sponsorship of the Division of Confucius Institute Affairs invited the Chargés d affaires Lv Jian, Ms. Narisara Chavaltanpipat, Deputy Education Minister of Thailand, and Zhang Xiangyang, Deputy Director of Education Commission of Chinese Tianjin Municipality, to unveil the bronze statue and attended the launch ceremony for the two books commemorating the 5th Anniversary of the Confucius Classroom: On the Common Enterprise and Master Zhaokun Thongchai & Tianjin and the launch ceremony of the "Happy China Tour" Chinese teaching website.

Chargés d affaires Lv Jian stated that the Confucius Classroom at Traimitwittayalai High School, as the world's first Confucius Classroom, has carried out various Chinese cultural activities, such as the Chinese Bridge Chinese Proficiency Competition, the compilation of the "Happy China Tour" textbooks as well as offering Chinese cultural curricula which have started a new era in the teaching of Chinese and Sino-Thai cultural exchange. Confucianism has a great influence on China and the world; the Confucius Institute and Confucius Classroom have become a cultural brand of China as well as being messengers linking the cultural exchanges between China and the world. The unveiling ceremony for the Confucius bronze statue is of special significance. Lv Jian also expressed the hope that the Confucius Classroom would make full use of its merits to become a pioneer in the dissemination of Chinese culture.

Chargés d'affaires Lv Jian mentioned in his address that since 1975, frequent exchanges between high level leaders of the two (2) countries have injected fresh vigor into the lasting, comprehensive and in-depth development of bilateral relations. The two (2) countries have made significant achievements in friendly exchanges across various spheres over the past 35 years. In recent years, Chinese education has become a highlight of the two sides' cooperation. As the world's first Confucius Classroom, the Confucius Classroom at Traimitwittayalai High School has been committed to promotion of Chinese language and culture through all kinds of means and has boosted the development of the friendship between the two peoples under the leadership of Master Zhaokun Thongchai, chairman of the Thai Council of the Confucius Classroom. Lv also hopes that the celebrations help people in Thailand to understand China further in order to aid Sino-Thai friendship in enduring generation after generation.

Over recent years, the Confucius Institutes' development has been sharped and they have provided scope for people all over the world to learn about Chinese language and culture. In addition they have become a platform for cultural exchanges between China and the world as well as a bridge reinforcing friendship and cooperation between China and the rest of the world and are much welcomed across the globe. Through the joint efforts of China and the Confucius Institute host countries in addition to the enthusiasm and active support of people all over the world, by the end of 2010, there have been 322 Confucius Institutes and 369 Confucius Classrooms established in 96 countries. In addition, some 250 institutions from over 50 countries have expressed requirements for establishing Confucius Institutes/Classrooms, among them some of the world's top universities.

Confucius Institutes/Classrooms adopt flexible teaching patterns and adapt to suit local conditions when teaching Chinese language and promoting culture in foreign primary schools, secondary schools, communities and enterprises. In 2009, Confucius Institutes/Classrooms around the world offered 9,000 Chinese courses of multitude styles, with a total enrollment of 260,000, a 130,000 strong enrollment increase from the previous year. More than 7,500 cultural exchange activities took place, involving the participation of over 3 million reaching double the participation figures of the corresponding period from the previous year.

Based on the Traimit Model of Education, the Confucius Classroom at Traimittwittayalai High School has offered training courses and organized international Chinese competition known as the "Chinese Language Bridge-Top Crown Diamond Cup." This competition has attracted over 32,500 competitors and professionals as model of Chinese and foreign educational cooperation. The 32 volumes of Happy Travel in China series of textbooks which are developed with the cooperation of Tianjin Experimental High School, have been widely used by more than 10,000 students in Thailand. It organized book exhibitions and the Hanban donated high-tech function school facilities and equipment for the first Confucius Classroom.

E. One Belt One Road : Universal Perspectives in World Peace and Development through Change, Innovation, Idealism and Freedom

The philosophical wisdom for world peace reflects the simple way to express that "Every day the world turns to break the new day." The element of time embodies the essence of life. This reflects the changing world where the gradual transformation of everyday activities that defines the life cycle of mankind. However, the most interesting struggle of the life cycle defines by how we govern, how we dictate the kind of goods and services, how we follow our beliefs, ideals and aspirations, and how we weave the knowledge and love we have to live in this beautiful world.

The new day demonstrates the changing perspectives on how we aspire and live our life working harmoniously to attain world peace and development for our future. Basically, we consider these life cycles of the new day to embrace the development of world peace through change, innovation, idealism and freedom. These are within the clauses of noble truths where Buddhism defines the essence of life from its conception of suffering to the cessation of the gradual path that may follow within the gradual wisdom steps of change, innovation, idealism and freedom. The "One Road One Belt" describes the paradigm shift for world peace that transforms the continuum process of change, innovation, idealism and freedom in the economic, technological, cultural and political development to attain the quality of life among the participating countries in the world. There are so much to learn in openness, oneness and inclusiveness in reminiscing the past grandeur of our great ancestors who guided us the role model in the diplomatic respect and trust as the purveyor of truth for the existence of the Maritime Silk Road.

In its historical account, it defined the diplomatic peace and unity in the major civilizations of Asia, Europe and Africa for thousands of years that resulted to the cultural assimilation and amalgamation of the Chinese people among the different nations of the world to the contemporary time. This symbolizes the closeness of human hearts and spirits to bring world peace even in the 21st century. The Maritime Silk Road which is the basis of the "One Belt One Road," it evolves as a good model of political and economic life which the Asian nations respected the ideas of wholesome development of the society where independence and freedom existed vis-à-vis to technological innovations. The sovereign states transformed into dynamic and vibrant economic order with good diplomatic ties among Asian nations . In contemporary time, this has been achieved by the industrialized states of Asia. However, the political and economic philosophy may be different from the western nations but the genuine principles are still reflective in its underlying principles of the quality of life in the Asian region.

The idea of world peace must always bring the principles of peaceful co-existence within the ambit of amity and comity through interdependence of the sovereign states. The implementation of "One Belt One Road" can be extracted from the principles of the paradigm shift for World Peace and Development in the ideas of the President Xi Jinping that discusses the features of the change, innovation, idealism and freedom. Basically, the diplomacy strategy is to apply the regional cooperation for bilateral and multilateral agreements among the countries of the world. Likewise, the realignment of the development agenda and thrusts of the sovereign nations are anchored on the quality of life that can be articulated in employment generation, poverty reduction, universal education, cultural diversity, technological and infrastructure economic support, and other means to enhance the productivity in the macro-level that be cascaded in the masses.

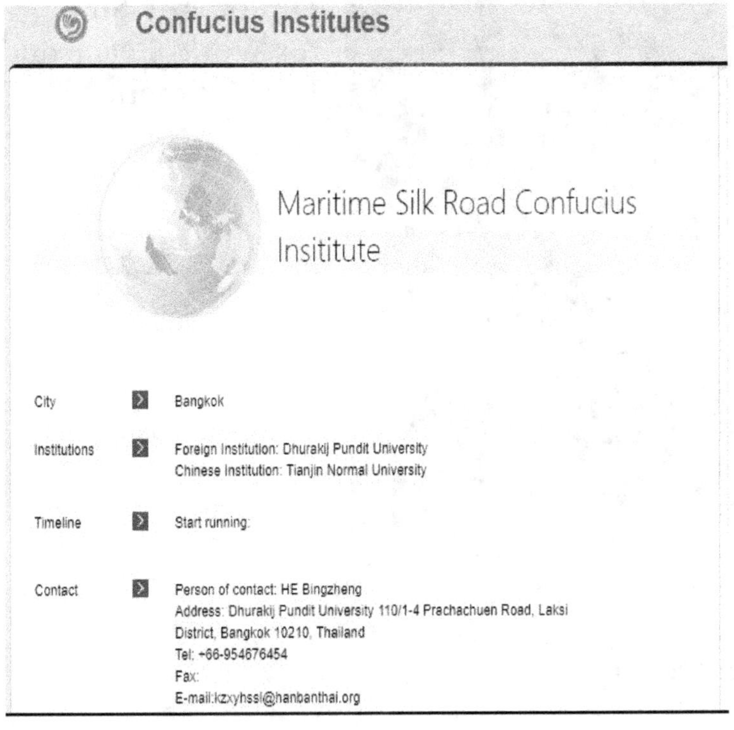

Appendix "A"

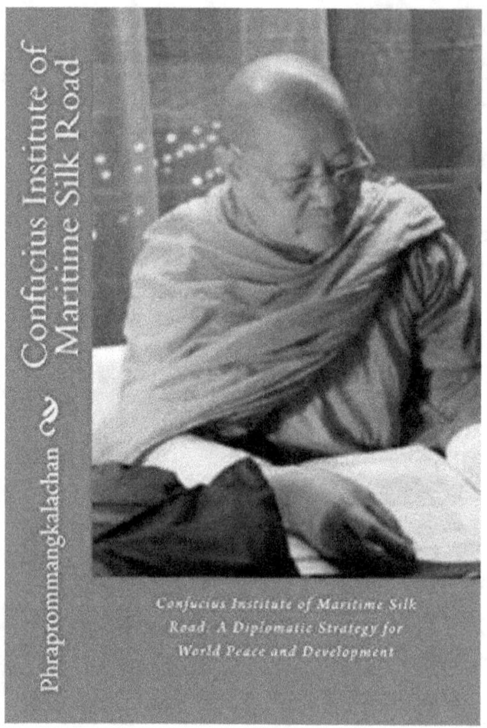

Confucius Institute of Maritime Silk Road: A Diplomatic Strategy for World Peace and Development

Product Website :

https://www.amazon.com/Confucius-Institute-Maritime-Silk-Road/dp/1517486084/ref=tmm_pap_title_0?_encoding=UTF8&qid=&sr

Product Details :

- **Paperback:** 170 pages
- **Publisher:** CreateSpace Independent Publishing Platform (September 23, 2015)
- **Language:** English
- **ISBN-10:** 1517486084
- **ISBN-13:** 978-1517486082
- **Product Dimensions:** 6 x 0.4 x 9 inches

Appendix "B"

Traimit Educational Model for the First Confucius School in Thailand

Product Website

https://www.amazon.com/Traimit-Educational-Confucius-School-Thailand

Product Details

- **Paperback:** 146 pages
- **Publisher:** CreateSpace Independent Publishing Platform (September 23, 2015)
- **Language:** English
- **ISBN-10:** 1517488745
- **ISBN-13:** 978-1517488741
- **Product Dimensions:** 6 x 0.3 x 9 inches

Appendix "C"

One Belt One Road : Universal Perspectives in World Peace and Development through Change, Innovation, Idealism and Freedom

Product Website

https://www.amazon.com/One-Belt-Road-Perspectives-Development/dp/154042541X/ref=la_B01N31YJIP_1_2?s=books&ie=UTF8&qid=1509712090&sr=1-2

Product details

- **Paperback:** 144 pages
- **Publisher:** CreateSpace Independent Publishing Platform (November 15, 2016)
- **Language:** English
- **ISBN-10:** 154042541X
- **ISBN-13:** 978-1540425416
- **Product Dimensions:** 6 x 0.3 x 9 inches

Appendix "D"

Agreement on Establishing Maritime Silk Road Confucius Institute Branch Officially Signed

[Source]　Thailand Maritime Silk Road Confucius Institute
[Time]　2016-12-28 13:56:46
http://english.hanban.org/article/2016-12/28/content_670033.htm

On Dec. 13, authorized by Confucius Institute Headquarters (Hanban), Master Phraprommangkalachan, Thailand Chairman of the Maritime Silk Road Confucius Institute Board of Directors, Pong Horadal, President of Phranakhon Rajabhat University and Zhang Qiaogui, President of Dali University jointly signed the agreement on establishing the Maritime Silk Road Confucius Institute at Phranakhon Rajabhat University.

Meeting site

The Maritime Silk Road Confucius Institute at Phranakhon Rajabhat University is a subordinate institute established in accordance with the development of situation and work demand of the Maritime Silk Road Confucius Institute. As an institute with relatively independent operation, the Maritime Silk Road Confucius Institute at Phranakhon Rajabhat University will run under the guidance of Maritime Silk Road Confucius

Institute, complete the tasks assigned by it and be incorporated into the its overall development framework.

The three parties signing cooperation agreements.

At the signing ceremony, Phranakhon Rajabhat University and Dali University expressed that the establishment of the Maritime Silk Road Confucius Institute at Phranakhon Rajabhat University is the mission endowed by the times. They will make a good start and devote unremitting efforts to improving the level of Chinese teaching, expanding cultural exchanges, enhancing the friendship between the two peoples and cultivating qualified people for the two countries and societies.

Phranakhon Rajabhat University is the first university in Thailand to train teachers, and now it is a university with multiple subjects including education, management, humanities and industrial technology. Leading in medicine, pharmacy, pedagogy, and biology, and featuring ethnology and art, Dali University is a comprehensive university with multidisciplinary integration and multi-level coordinated development. The two universities have enjoyed friendly cooperation for years, and are practice bases of Chinese and Thai teaching for each other.

Appendix "E"
Maritime Silk Road Confucius Institute in Thailand and Rayong Industrial Zone Sign Strategic Cooperative Partnership Agreement

[Source] Confucius Institute Headquarters (Hanban)
[Time]　2017-09-13 17:44:09
http://english.hanban.org/article/2017-09/13/content_698811.htm
Photos by Sun Guangyong

Delegates from the Maritime Silk Road Confucius Institute in Thailand and Rayong Industrial Zone jointly signing a strategic cooperative partnership agreement

On September 9th local time, the Joint Conference of Asian Confucius Institutes along the Belt and Road was held in Bangkok Thailand, attracting a total of 250 representatives from all the 77 Confucius Institutes and 14 Confucius Classrooms in the 30 countries along the route, relevant Chinese universities and educational institutions in other countries, the Chinese Embassy in Thailand, relevant governmental departments of Thailand and Chinese-funded enterprises to attend the conference.

As of now, the Confucius Institute Headquarters has set up 135 Confucius Institutes and 129 Confucius Classrooms in 51 countries among all the 64 countries along the "Belt and Road". Of all the Confucius Institutes and Confucius Classrooms, 77 institutes and 79 classrooms were set up in 30 Asian countries.

During the conference, the Confucius Institute and Thailand-China Rayong Industrial Zone signed a strategic cooperative partnership agreement. This is the institute's new measure to practice the Belt and Road Initiative. The Maritime Silk Road Confucius Institute at Phranakhon Rajabhat University, which is co-established by Dali University of China and Phranakhon Rajabhat University, will carry out the specific projects in the agreement.

The cooperation between the Maritime Silk Road Confucius Institute and Rayong Industrial Zone is not only a new attempt to respond to the Belt and Road Initiative, but also serves as a contributor to the construction of the Eastern Thailand Economic Corridor. The Confucius Institute will not only provide Chinese language training to executives and employees in Thailand and from other countries, but also actively implement China-Thailand cultural exchanges. By setting up vocational training platforms, the Confucius Institute can offer opportunities of internship, field practice and employment to students from both Chinese and Thai universities, so as to enhance educational, cultural, and economic and trade cooperation between China and Thailand.

Thailand-Chinese Rayong Industrial Zone is located in Rayong along the east coast of Thailand. It is now the largest Chinese industrial zone in Thailand, as well as Southeast Asia. Through 12-plus years' development, around one hundred Chinese enterprises have operated in the industrial zone, bringing about 30 million US dollars of Chinese investment to the Thai economy. At present, there are more than 6000 Chinese and around 30,000 Thais working in the industrial zone.

Appendix "F"

13th "Chinese Bridge-Diamond Crown Jewel" International Chinese Language Contest held in Bangkok

[Source]   Confucius Institute of Maritime Silk Road
[Time]   2016-09-28 12:21:31
http://english.hanban.org/article/2017-09/13/content_698811.htm
By Li Meng

On September 4th, the 13th "Chinese Bridge-Diamond Crown Jewel" International Chinese Language Contest was held at Dhurakij Pundit University in Bangkok. At this year's contest, directors of Confucius Institutes and Chinese heads of Confucius Classrooms in Bangkok and nearby regions as well as local experts on Chinese language teaching were invited as judges.

Around 4,000 contestants from Thailand, China and countries in Southeast Asia participated in the competition. Unlike previous contests, this year, organizers grouped the contestants into the Chinese category and non-Chinese category to ensure a fair competition.

Guests attending the opening ceremony of this contest included Master Phraprommangkalachan, President of Romchatra Foundation of Thailand, Chair of the Board of the Confucius Institute of Maritime Silk Road and Chairman of the Confucius Classroom at Traimit Wittayalai High School; Duriya Amatawiwat, Assistant to Vice Minister of Education of Thailand; Darika Lathapipat, Vice President of Dhurakij Pundit University; Zhou Gaoyu, First Secretary of the Education Office of the Chinese Embassy in Thailand; and also representatives of Confucius Institutes and Confucius Classrooms across Thailand.

In her congratulatory letter, Mdm. Xu Lin, Chief Executive of Confucius Institute Headquarters and Director General of Hanban, extended her warm congratulations to this event as well as sincere appreciation and great respect to Master Phraprommangkalachan for his concern and support for this event. Relevant Chinese universities including Dali University and Northwest Normal University also sent their congratulations to this event.

Duriya Amatawiwat addressing the event

On behalf of the Ministry of Education of Thailand, Duriya Amatawiwat spoke highly of the "Chinese Bridge-Diamond Crown Jewel" Contest and expressed her appreciation to all parties for their support for the Chinese language promotion and the development of education in Thailand. Darika Lathapipat noted that learning Chinese is of particular importance to better promoting exchange and mutual understanding between China and Thailand. The "Chinese Bridge-Diamond Crown Jewel" Contest not only serves as a platform for Thai students to learn Chinese, but also creates an arena for them to showcase themselves, strengthen their capabilities and broaden their horizons.

In his remarks, Mr. Zhou Gaoyu highly commended Master Phraprommangkalachan's contributions and hoped that the "Chinese Bridge-Diamond Crown Jewel" Contest, initiated by Master Phraprommangkalachan, would become a bridge of educational and cultural cooperation between not only China and Thailand but also China and ASEAN.

Master Phraprommangkalachan presenting certificates to prize winners

After the competition, Master Phraprommangkalachan presented the trophies granted by Crown Prince Maha Vajiralongkorn and Princess Maha Chakri Sirindhorn, certificates and Master Phraprommangkalachan scholarships as tokens of encouragement. He hoped that the contestants would make persistent efforts in their Chinese learning so as to become friendly envoys of cultural exchanges between Thailand and China and contribute to the social and economic development of Thailand.

A group photo of the guests, representatives from various social sectors and prize winners of the contest

The "Chinese Bridge-Diamond Crown Jewel" International Chinese Language Contest is an international Chinese language competition jointly hosted by the Confucius Institute of Maritime Silk Road, the Confucius Classroom at Traimit Wittayalai High School, Tianjin Experimental High School in China and Dhurakij Pundit University, with Romchatra Foundation of Thailand as the sponsor of scholarships. This contest, taking language competition as a major channel, aims at promoting cultural exchanges, deepening mutual understanding and encouraging Chinese language learners of various countries to make constant progress in their Chinese learning. In addition, this year's competition receives strong support from Chia Tai Group and Hainan Airlines.

Appendix "G"

Academic Collaboration with the Confucius Institute of Maritime Silk Road

Source : Sripatum International University

https://www.spu.ac.th/fac/intl/en/content.php?cid=774

President Dr. Rutchaneeporn P. Phukkamarn led SPU Executives, faculty members, staff and students to welcome Phra Prommangkalachan, Deputy Abbot of Traimitr Withayaram Woraviharn temple and Thailand Chairman of the Confucius Institute of Maritime Silk Road, to Sripatum University main campus in Bangkok on 16 November 2016. The main purpose of this visit was to sign the Memorandum of Understanding between Sripatum University and the Confucius Institute of Maritime Silk Road.

The MOU signing ceremony was held at the Exhibition Hall, Building 11, and the event was also attended by the Board of Directors from the Confucius Institute of Maritime Silk Road. This collaboration aims to support Sripatum University to become a leader for the education networking, to create collaborative academic activities such as training and seminar for the benefits of faculty members and students, and finally to give impetus for Thailand's Education to be developed and be at the top level in ASEAN.

Appendix "H"

Following is the full text of the keynote speech given by Chinese President Xi Jinping at the Boao Forum for Asia Annual Conference 2015: (Source : Ministry of Foreign Affairs of the People's Republic of China-http://www.fmprc.gov.cn/mfa_eng/wjdt_665385/zyjh_665391/t1250690.shtml)

Boao Forum for Asia Annual Conference 2015 Towards a Community of Common Destiny and A New Future for Asia

Keynote Speech by H.E. Xi Jinping
President of the People's Republic of China
At the Boao Forum for Asia Annual Conference 2015
Boao, 28 March 2015

Your Excellencies Heads of State and Government,

Ministers,

Heads of International and Regional Organizations,

Members of the Board of Directors of the Boao Forum for Asia,

Ladies and Gentlemen,

Dear Friends,

Boao today greets us with vast ocean, high sky and warm breeze. In this beautiful season of spring, it is of great significance that so many distinguished guests gather here to discuss the development strategies for

Asia and the world.

At the outset, let me extend, on behalf of the Chinese government and people and in my own name, heartfelt welcome to all the distinguished guests attending the Boao Forum for Asia Annual Conference2015, and my warm congratulations on the opening of the conference.

The theme of this year's conference is "Asia's New Future: Towards a Community of Common Destiny". The timing could not be better in that the theme has not only great immediate relevance but also long-term historical significance. And I am looking to all of you to express yourselves fully and contribute your insightful views to the cause of peace and development of Asia and beyond.

Ladies and Gentlemen,

Dear Friends,

There are certain historic occasions that are likely to remind people of what happened in the past and set people reflecting on them. This year marks the 70th anniversary of the end of the World Anti-Fascist War, the victory of the Chinese People's War of Resistance Against Japanese Aggression and the founding of the United Nations. This year is also the 60th anniversary of the Bandung Conference and will witness the completion of the ASEAN Community. As such, it is an important year to be commemorated as well as a historic juncture to reflect on the past and look to the future.

Over the past 70 years, the world has experienced profound changes as never before, making a difference to the destiny of mankind. With the days of global colonialism and the Cold War long gone, countries are now increasingly interconnected and interdependent. Peace, development and win-win cooperation have become the prevailing trend of our times. The international forces are shifting in a way that is more favorable to maintaining world peace. Countries are now in a better position to uphold general stability in the world and seek common development.

Over the past 70 years, Asia has also gone through unprecedented changes. After gaining national independence, Asian countries took their destiny in their own hands and strengthened the force for regional and world peace. Asian countries were the first to advocate the Five Principles of Peaceful Co-existence and, together with African countries, put forward the Ten Principles on handling state-to-state relations at the Bandung Conference. Since the end of the Cold War, Asian countries have gradually come up with an Asian way of cooperation in the course of advancing regional cooperation, which features mutual respect, consensus-building and accommodation of each other's comfort levels. All this has contributed to a proper approach to state-to-state relations and to progress in building a new type of international relations.

Over the past 70 years, more and more Asian countries have found development paths that suit their own national conditions and embarked on a fast-track of economic growth. Having emerged from poverty and backwardness, they are on course to achieve development and prosperity. Regional and inter-regional cooperation is flourishing. Connectivity is pursued at a faster pace. As a result, there is a strong momentum in Asia with countries striving to outperform each other. Accounting for one third of the world economy, Asia is one of the most dynamic regions with the most potential and its global strategic importance has been rising.

Over the past 70 years, Asian countries have gradually transcended their differences in ideology and social system. No longer cut off from each other, they are now open and inclusive, with suspicion and estrangement giving way to growing trust and appreciation. The interests of Asian countries have become intertwined, and a community of common destiny has increasingly taken shape. Be it the arduous struggle for national independence, or the difficult periods of the Asian financial crisis and the international financial crisis, or the hard time in the wake of devastating disasters including the Indian Ocean tsunami and earthquake in Wenchuan, China, the people of Asian countries have always come to those in need with a helping hand and worked together to overcome one challenge after another, demonstrating the power of unity in face of difficulties and the spirit of sharing weal and woe. This said, Asia still faces numerous challenges. Some are the old issues left over from history and others are new ones associated with current disputes. Asia is also confronted with various traditional and non-traditional security threats. Hence it remains an uphill battle for Asian countries to grow the economy, improve people's livelihood and eliminate poverty.

A review of the path traversed over the past 70 years shows that what has been accomplished in Asia today is attributable to the persistent efforts of several generations of people in Asian countries and to the hard work of many statesmen and people of great vision. Tomorrow, Singapore will hold a state funeral for Mr. Lee Kuan Yew. Mr. Lee was a strategist and statesman respected across the world for his outstanding contribution to the peace and development of Asia and the exchanges and cooperation between Asia and the world. I want to take this opportunity to pay high tribute to Mr. Lee Kuan Yew and all those who made contribution to Asia's peace and development.

Ladies and Gentlemen,

Dear Friends,

Asia belongs to the world. For Asia to move towards a community of common destiny and embrace a new future, it has to follow the world trend and seek progress and development in tandem with that of the world.

The international situation continues to experience profound and complex changes, with significant development in multipolarization and economic globalization. Cultural diversity and IT application are making constant progress while readjustment is accelerating in international landscape and order. Countries around the world are losing no time in adjusting their development strategies, pursuing transformation and innovation, changing their economic development models, improving economic structures and opening up new horizons for further development. At the same time, however, the world economy is still in a period of profound adjustment, with risks of low growth, low inflation and low demand interwoven with risks of high unemployment, high debt and high level of bubbles. The performance and policies of major economies continue to diverge, and uncertainties in the economic climate remain prominent. Geopolitical factors are more at play and local turmoils keep cropping up. Non-traditional security threats and global challenges including terrorism, cyber security, energy security, food security, climate change and major infectious diseases are on the rise, and the North-South gap is still wide. The noble cause of peace and development remains a long and arduous journey for mankind.

We have only one planet, and countries share one world. To do well, Asia and the world could not do without each other. Facing the fast changing international and regional landscapes, we must see the whole picture, follow the trend of our times and jointly build a regional order that is more favorable to Asia and the world. We should, through efforts towards such a community for Asia, promote a community of common interest for all mankind. I wish to take this opportunity to share with you my thoughts on this vision.

-- To build a community of common destiny, we need to make sure that all countries respect one another and treat each other as equals. Countries may differ in size, strength or level of development, but they are all equal members of the international community with equal rights to participate in regional and international affairs. On matters that involve us all, we should discuss and look for a solution together. Being a big country means shouldering greater responsibilities for regional and world peace and development, as opposed to seeking greater monopoly over regional and world affairs.

To respect one another and treat each other as equals, countries need to, first and foremost, respect other countries' social systems and development paths of their own choice, respect each other's core interests and major concerns and have objective and rational perception of other countries' growing strength, policies and visions. Efforts should be made to seek common ground while shelving differences, and better still to increase common interests and dissolve differences. The hard-won peace and stability in Asia and the sound momentum for development should be upheld by all. All of us must oppose interference in other countries' internal affairs and reject attempts to destablize the region out of selfish motives.

-- To build a community of common destiny, we need to seek win-win cooperation and common development. Our friends in Southeast Asia say that the lotus flowers grow taller as the water rises. Our friends in Africa say that if you want to go fast, walk alone; and if you want to go far, walk together. Our friends in Europe say that a single tree cannot block the chilly wind. And Chinese people say that when big rivers have water, the small ones are filled; and when small rivers have water, the big ones are filled. All these sayings speak to one same truth, that is, only through win win cooperation can we make big and sustainable achievements that are beneficial to all. The old mindset of zero-sum game should give way to a new approach of win-win and all-win cooperation. The interests of others must be accommodated while pursuing one's own interests, and common development must be promoted while seeking one's own development. The vision of win-win cooperation not only applies to the economic field, but also to the political, security, cultural and many other fields. It not only applies to countries within the region, but also to cooperation with countries from outside the region. We should enhance coordination of macroeconomic policies to prevent negative spill-over effects that may arise from economic policy changes in individual economies. We should actively promote reform of global economic governance, uphold an open world economy, and jointly respond to risks and challenges in the world economy.

China and ASEAN countries will join hands in building an even closer China-ASEAN community of common destiny. The building of an East Asia economic community for ASEAN, China, Japan and ROK will be completed in 2020. We should actively build a free trade cooperation network in Asia and strive to conclude negotiations on an upgraded China ASEAN FTA and on Regional Comprehensive Economic Partnership (RCEP) in 2015. In advancing economic integration in Asia, we need to stay committed to open regionalism and move forward trans-regional cooperation, including APEC, in a coordinated manner.

We will vigorously promote a system of regional financial cooperation, explore a platform for exchanges and cooperation among Asian financial institutions, and advance complementary and coordinated development between the Asian Infrastructure Investment Bank (AIIB) and such multilateral financial institutions as the Asian Development Bank and the World Bank. We will strengthen practical cooperation in currency stability, investment and financing, and credit rating, make progress in institution building for the Chiang Mai Initiative Multilateralization and build a regional financial security network. We will work towards an energy and resources cooperation mechanism in Asia to ensure energy and resources security.

China proposes that plans be formulated regarding connectivity building in East Asia and Asia at large to advance full integration in infrastructure, policies and institutions and personnel flow. We may increase maritime connectivity, speed up institution building for marine cooperation in Asia, and step up cooperation in marine economy, environmental protection, disaster management and fishery. This way, we could turn the seas of Asia into seas of peace, friendship and cooperation for Asian countries.

-- To build a community of common destiny, we need to pursue common, comprehensive, cooperative and sustainable security. In today's world, security means much more than before and its implications go well beyond a single region or time frame. All sorts of factors could have a bearing on a country's security. As people of all countries share common destiny and become increasingly interdependent, no country could have its own security ensured without the security of other countries or of the wider world. The Cold War mentality should truly be discarded and new security concepts be nurtured as we explore a path for Asia that ensures security for all, by all and of all.

We believe that countries are all entitled to take an equal part in regional security affairs and all are obliged to work to ensure security for the region. The legitimate security concerns of each country need to be respected and addressed. At the same time, in handling security issues in Asia, itis important to bear in mind both the history and reality of Asia, take a multi-pronged and holistic approach, improve coordinated regional security governance, and safeguard security in both the traditional and nontraditional realms. It is important to conduct dialogue and cooperation to enhance security at national and regional levels, and to increase cooperation as the way to safeguard peace and security. It is important to resolve disputes through peaceful means, and oppose the willful use or threat of force. Security should be given equal emphasis as development, and sustainable development surely provides a way to sustainable security. Countries in Asia need to step up cooperation with countries and organizations outside the region and all parties are welcome to play a positive and constructive role in upholding development and security in Asia.

-- To build a community of common destiny, we need to ensure inclusiveness and mutual learning among civilizations. History, over the past millennia, has witnessed ancient civilizations appear and thrive along the Yellow and Yangtze Rivers, the Indus, the Ganges, the Euphrates, and the Tigris River as well as in Southeast Asia, each adding its own splendour to the progress of human civilization. Today, Asia has proudly maintained its distinct diversity and still nurtures all the civilizations, ethnic groups and religions in this big Asian family.

Mencius, the great philosopher in ancient China, said, "Things are born to be different. "Civilizations are only unique, and no one is superior to the other. There need to be more exchange and dialogue among civilizations and development models, so that each could draw on the strength of the other and all could thrive and prosper by way of mutual learning and common development. Let us promote inter-civilization exchanges to build bridges of friendship for our people, drive human development and safeguard peace of the world.

China proposes that a conference of dialogue among Asian civilizations be held to provide a platform upon which to enhance interactions among the youth, people's groups, local communities and the media and to form a network of think-tank cooperation, so as to add to Asian people's rich cultural life and contribute to more vibrant regional cooperation and development.

Ladies and Gentlemen,

Dear Friends,

Right now, the Chinese people are working in unison under the strategic plans to complete the building of a moderately prosperous society in all respects, and to comprehensively deepen reform, advance law-based governance, and enforce strict Party conduct. Our objective is to realize the "two centenary" goals for China's development and for realizing the Chinese dream of great national rejuvenation. I wish to use this opportunity to reaffirm China's commitment to the path of peaceful development, and to promoting cooperation and common development in the Asia-Pacific.

China will be firm in its determination and resolve and all its policies will be designed to achieve such a purpose.

Now, the Chinese economy has entered a state of new normal. It is shifting gear from high speed to medium-to-high speed growth, from an extensive model that emphasized scale and speed to a more intensive one emphasizing quality and efficiency, and from being driven by investment in production factors to being driven by innovation. China's economy grew by 7.4% in 2014, with 7% increase in labor productivity and 4.8% decrease in energy intensity. The share of domestic consumption in GDP rose, the services sector expanded at a faster pace, and the economy's efficiency and quality continued to improve. When looking at China's economy, one should not focus on growth rate only. As the economy continues to grow in size, around 7% growth would be quite impressive, and the momentum it generates would be larger than growth at double digits in previous years. It is fair to say that the Chinese economy is highly resilient and has much potential, which gives us enough room to leverage a host of policy tools. Having said that, China will continue to be responsive to the new trend and take initiatives to shape the new normal in our favor. We will focus on improving quality and efficiency, and give even greater priority to shifting the growth model and adjusting the structure of development. We will make more solid efforts to boost economic development and deepen reform and opening-up. We will take more initiatives to unleash the creativity and ingenuity of the people, be more effective in safeguarding equity and social justice, raise people's living standards and make sure that China's economic and social development are both sound and stable.

This new normal of the Chinese economy will continue to bring more opportunities of trade, growth, investment and cooperation for other countries in Asia and beyond. In the coming five years, China will import more than US$10 trillion of goods, Chinese investment abroad will exceed US$500 billion, and more than 500 million outbound visits will be made by Chinese tourists. China will stick to its basic state policy of opening up, improve its investment climate, and protect the lawful rights and interests of investors. I believe that together, the people of Asian countries could drive this train of Asia's development to take Asia to an even brighter future.

What China needs most is a harmonious and stable domestic environment and a peaceful and tranquil international environment. Turbulence or war runs against the fundamental interests of the Chinese people. The Chinese nation loves peace and has, since ancient times, held high such philosophies that "harmony is the most valuable", "peace and harmony should prevail" and "all men under heaven are brothers". China has suffered from turbulence and war for more than a century since modern times, and the Chinese people would never want to inflict the same tragedy on other countries or peoples. History has taught us that no country who tried to achieve its goal with force ever succeeded. China will be steadfast in pursuing the independent foreign policy of peace, the path of peaceful development, the win-win strategy of opening-up, and the approach of upholding justice while pursuing shared interests. China will work to promote a new type of international relations of win-win cooperation and will always remain a staunch force for world peace and common development.

Close neighbors are better than distant relatives. This is a simple truth that the Chinese people got to know in ancient times. That explains China's firm commitment to building friendship and partnership with its neighbors to foster an amicable, secure and prosperous neighborhood. Under the principle of amity, sincerity, mutual benefit and inclusiveness, China is working actively to deepen win-win cooperation and connectivity with its neighbors to bring them even more benefit with its own development. China has signed treaties of good-neighborliness, friendship and cooperation with eight of its neighbors and is holding discussion to sign a same treaty with ASEAN. China stands ready to sigh such a treaty with all its neighbors to provide strong support for the development of bilateral relations as well as prosperity and stability in the region.

In 2013, during my visit to Kazakhstan and Indonesia, I put forward the initiatives of building a Silk Road economic belt and a 21st century maritime Silk Road. The "Belt and Road" initiative, meeting the development needs of China, countries along the routes and the region at large, will serve the common interests of relevant parties and answer the call of our time for regional and global cooperation.

In promoting this initiative, China will follow the principle of wide consultation, joint contribution and shared benefits. The programs of development will be open and inclusive, not exclusive. They will be a real chorus comprising all countries along the routes, not a solo for China itself. To develop the Belt and Road is not to replace existing mechanisms or initiatives for regional cooperation. Much to the contrary, we will build on the existing basis to help countries align their development strategies and form complementarity. Currently, more than 60 countries along the routes and international organizations have shown interest in taking part in the development of the Belt and the Road. The "Belt and Road" and the AIIB are both open initiatives. We welcome all countries along the routes and in Asia, as well as our friends and partners around the world, to take an active part in these endeavors.

The "Belt and Road" initiative is not meant as rhetoric. It represents real work that could be seen and felt to bring real benefits to countries in the region. Thanks to the concerted efforts of relevant parties, the vision and action paper of the initiative has been developed. Substantive progress has been made in the establishment of the AIIB. The Silk Road Fund has been launched, and constructions of a number of infrastructure connectivity projects are moving forward. These early harvests have truly pointed to the broad prospects the "Belt and Road" initiative will bring.

Ladies and Gentlemen,

Dear Friends,

The cause of peace and development of mankind is as lofty as its is challenging. The journey ahead will not be smooth sailing, and success may not come easily. No matter how long and difficult the journey may be, those who work together and never give up will eventually prevail. I believe that as long as we keep to our goals and make hard efforts, we will together bring about a community of common destiny and usher in a new future for Asia.

I wish the Annual Conference a complete success.

Thank you very much.

Appendix "I"

Speech by Chinese President Xi Jinping to Indonesian Parliament

(2 October 2013, Jakarta, Indonesia)
Source: ASEAN-China Centre
Time: 2013-Oct-3 15:48
Website : http://www.asean-china-center.org/english/201310/03/c_133062675.htm

Dear Friends, Apa Kabar! Good morning. It gives me great pleasure to come to the People's Representative Council of Indonesia and meet all the friends here. I am visiting Indonesia, known as "country of thousands islands", at the invitation of President Susilo Bambang Yudhoyono. This is the first leg in my current visit to Southeast Asia. It is a journey for carrying forward traditional friendship and also for planning future cooperation.

I visited Indonesia 20 years ago, during which I personally experienced the development, colorful scenery and diversified culture of Indonesia. How time flies. But what I saw 20 years ago is still vivid in my mind, as if it only happened yesterday. As I set foot on this beautiful land again this time, I am even more impressed by the robust vitality of our bilateral relations and the profound friendship between the two peoples. In recent years, under the leadership of President Yudhoyono, the Indonesian people have pulled together, made tremendous efforts and achieved success in economic development, social stability and growing national strength. I sincerely wish the Indonesian people further success in forging a better future through hard work and creativity.

Ladies and Gentlemen: Dear Friends, China and Indonesia face each other across the sea. The friendly ties between us have a long history. Together, our peoples have composed one piece after another of beautiful music about their exchanges and interactions over the centuries. Just as the Indonesian folk song Bengawan Solo, a household musical piece in China, goes "Your water springs forth from Solo, caged by a thousand mountains. Water flows to reach far distances, eventually to the sea." Like the beautiful river Solo, China-Indonesia relations have traversed an extraordinary journey, past mountains and eventually to the sea. As early as the Han Dynasty in China about 2,000 years ago, the people of the two countries opened the door to each other despite the sea between them. In the early 15th century, Zheng He, the famous Chinese navigator of the Ming Dynasty, made seven voyages to the Western Seas. He stopped over the

Indonesian archipelago in each of his voyages and toured Java, Sumatra and Kalimantan. His visits left nice stories of friendly exchanges between the Chinese and Indonesian peoples, many of which are still widely told today.

Over the centuries, the vast oceans have served as the bond of friendship connecting the two peoples, not a barrier between them. Vessels full of goods and passengers travelled across the sea, exchanging products and fostering friendship. A Dream of Red Mansions, a Chinese classic novel, gives vivid accounts of rare treasures from Java. The National Museum of Indonesia, on the other hand, displays a large number of ancient Chinese porcelains. All these bear witness to the friendly exchanges between the two peoples. And they are convincing interpretation of the Chinese saying that "A bosom friend afar brings a distant land near." Our two peoples sympathized with and supported each other in their respective struggle for national independence and liberation in the last century. Indonesia was among the first countries to establish diplomatic ties with the People's Republic of China after its founding in 1949. In 1955, China and Indonesia, together with other Asian and African countries, jointly initiated the Bandung spirit at the Bandung Conference. With the principles of peaceful coexistence and seeking common ground while shelving differences at its core, the Bandung spirit remains an important norm governing state-to-state relations, and has made indelible contribution to the building of new international relations. Our two countries resumed diplomatic ties in 1990 and established a strategic partnership in 2005, which marked the start of a new phase in the growth of our bilateral relations.

Ladies and Gentlemen: Dear Friends, During my current visit, President Yudhoyono and I have jointly announced our decision to upgrade our bilateral relations to a comprehensive strategic partnership, with a view to building on past achievements and bringing about all-round and in-depth growth of our relationship. The growing mutual trust between the two countries has put our bilateral relations on a more solid political basis. Our practical cooperation has expanded from such traditional areas as economy, trade, finance, infrastructure, energy, resources and manufacturing to include new fields such as space and maritime affairs. Our wide-ranging cooperation, from space to ocean, has delivered tangible benefits to the two peoples. The Surabaya –Madura Bridge, a China Indonesia joint project, is the longest cross-sea bridge in Southeast Asia. The cooperation project of Jatigede Dam is about to finish. Once completed, it will have an irrigation area of 90,000 hectares, which will greatly facilitate the work and life of the local people. We have enhanced our cooperation on major regional and international issues. Our relations have increasingly gained regional and international influences. All this is of positive significance to the building of a more just and equitable international political and economic order. All these are important landmarks of China-Indonesia friendship in the new era.

People in Indonesia often say, "It's easy to make money but difficult to make friends." The sincere friendship between the Chinese and Indonesian people is indeed our cherished, priceless treasure. On 26 December 2004, a sudden massive earthquake of magnitude 9 hit the once tranquil Indian Ocean and triggered a large tsunami. The whole world was shocked to see Aceh of Indonesia suffering huge losses of life and property. After the tsunami, China immediately activated the emergency response mechanism and announced on the day of the earthquake that it would provide assistance to Indonesia and other disaster-affected countries. It became the largest overseas rescue and relief operation that China had ever launched after the founding of the People's Republic. Trucks carrying relief supplied were given green lights all the way and rushed from factories to airport, and airplanes, loaded with the love and sympathy of the Chinese people toward the Indonesian people, flew to Aceh and other disaster-hit areas. The Chinese international rescue team was the first foreign team to arrive at Aceh. They provided medical treatment to over 10,000 victims in a short span of 13 days. Many local people learned to speak Chinese and hailed members of the Chinese rescue team in Chinese, "zhongguo, beijing, wo ai ni"(China, Beijing, I love you.)

The Chinese people, too, offered their sympathy and assistance in a variety of ways to the Indonesia people hit by the disaster. An old man in Hangzhou, who was not rich himself as his wife was hospitalized for a long time and he himself had just gone through a surgery, donated 1,000 yuan of his hard earned money to Indonesian kids in disaster-affected areas for their continued schooling. The donation, though not a bit sum, speaks to the profound goodwill of the Chinese people to the Indonesian people. Likewise, the Indonesian people have extended a helping hand when the Chinese people experienced major natural disasters. On 12 May 2008, a massive earthquake hit Wenchuan, China. People in the affected areas were in dire need of assistance and relief. Indonesia responded immediately and sent its medical team to quake-hit areas. As soon as it arrived, the Indonesian medical team worked around the clock in spite of the many aftershocks. They treated 260 earthquake victims and provided free medical treatment to 844 local residents and 120 students. Before returning to Indonesia, they donated all their valuable belongings to the quake-affected areas. Back in Indonesia, people made donations both in cash and kind to the quake-stricken Wenchuan. Some Indonesians personally visited the Chinese Embassy in Indonesia to express their prayers and blessings to the people in Wenchuan. What they did has deeply moved the Chinese people.

There are countless touching stories like these about friendly ties between our peoples. They are all examples of what is captured by one common proverb in both the Chinese and Indonesian languages, namely "going through thick and thin together".

Ladies and Gentlemen: Dear Friends, China and ASEAN countries are linked by common mountains and rivers and share a historical bond. This year marks the tenth anniversary of the China-ASEAN strategic partnership. Our relationship now stands at a new historical starting point. China places great importance on Indonesia's status and influence in ASEAN. China wishes to work with Indonesia and other ASEAN countries to ensure that China and ASEAN are good neighbors, good friends and good partners who would share prosperity and security and stick together through thick and thin. By making joint efforts, we will build a more closely-knit China-ASEAN community of common destiny so as to bring more benefits to both China and ASEAN and to the people in the region. To that end, we should focus our efforts in the following areas:

First, build trust and develop good-neighborliness. Trust in the very foundation of both interpersonal and state-to-state relations. China is committed to a relationship of sincerity and friendship with ASEAN countries and to enhanced mutual political and strategic trust. There is no one-size-fits-all development model in the world or an unchanging development path. Both the Chinese people and people in ASEAN countries have embraced change and innovation with an open mind, and explored and found, in a pioneering and enterprising spirit, development paths in light of their specific national conditions that conform to the trend of times. All these efforts have opened up a broad prospect for their economic and social development. We should respect each other's right to independently choose social system and development path as well as each other's efforts to explore and pursue economic and social development, and improve people's lives. We should have full confidence in each other's strategic direction, support each other on issues of major concern, and never deviate from the general direction of China- ASEAN strategic cooperation. China is ready to discuss with ASEAN countries the prospect of concluding of a treaty of good-neighborliness, friendship and cooperation in a joint effort to build good-neighborly relations. China will continue to support ASEAN in growing its strength, building ASEAN community and playing a central role in regional cooperation.

Second, work for win-win cooperation. As a well-known Chinese saying goes, "The interests to be considered should be the interests of all," China is ready to open itself wider to ASEAN countries on the basis of equality and mutual benefit to enable ASEAN countries to benefit more from China's development. China is prepared to upgrade the China ASEAN Free Trade Area and strive to expand two-way trade to one trillion US dollars by 2020. China is committed to greater connectivity with ASEAN countries. China will propose the establishment of an Asian infrastructure investment bank that would give priority to ASEAN countries' needs. Southeast Asia has since ancient times been an important hub along the ancient Maritime Silk Road. China will strengthen maritime cooperation with ASEAN countries to make good use of the China ASEAN Maritime Cooperation Fund set up by the Chinese government and vigorously develop maritime partnership in a joint effort to build the Maritime Silk Road of the 21st century. China is ready to expand its practical cooperation with ASEAN countries across the board, supplying each other's needs and complementing each other's strengths, with a view to jointly seizing opportunities and meeting challenges for the benefit of common development and prosperity.

Third, stand together and assist each other. China and ASEAN countries are as close as lips and teeth. We share the responsibility for regional peace and stability. Historically, the people of China and ASEAN countries had stood together through thick and thin in the fight to take our destiny back into our own hands. In recent years, our peoples have stood side by side and forged strong synergy in responding to various crises from Asian financial crisis to the international financial crisis, and from the Indian Ocean tsunami to China's Wenchuan earthquake. We should cast away the Cold War mentality, champion the new thinking of comprehensive security, common security and cooperative security and jointly uphold regional peace and stability. We should deepen cooperation in disaster prevention and relief, cyber security, combating cross-border crimes and joint law enforcement to create a more peaceful, tranquil and amicable home for the people in the region. China is ready to work with ASEAN countries to improve China-ASEAN defense ministers' meeting mechanism and hold regular dialogues on regional security issues. With regard to differences and disputes between China and some Southeast Asian nations on territorial sovereignty and maritime rights and interests, peaceful solutions should be sought, and differences and disputes should be properly handled through equal-footed dialogue and friendly consultation in the overall interests of bilateral ties and regional stability.

Fourth, enhance mutual understanding and friendship. Just as a Chinese saying goes, "A big tree grows from a small seedling; and a nine storeyed tower is built out of soil." To ensure that the tree of China ASEAN friendship remains evergreen, the soil of social support for our relations should be compacted. Last year saw 15 million people traveling between China and ASEAN countries with over 1,000 flights between the two sides each week. Increased interactions have nurtured deeper bonds between us and enabled our people to feel ever closer to each other. We should encourage more friendly exchanges between youth, think tanks, parliaments, NGOs and civil organizations of the two sides, which in turn will generate more intellectual support to the growth of China-ASEAN relations and help increase the mutual understanding and friendship between our peoples. China is ready to send more volunteers to ASEAN countries to support their cultural, educational, health and medical development. China has proposed to set 2014 as the year of China-ASEAN cultural exchanges. In the coming three to five years, china will offer ASEAN countries 15,000 government scholarships.

Fifth, stick to openness and inclusiveness. The sea is big because it admits all rivers. In the long course of human history, the people of China and ASEAN countries have created splendid and great civilizations renowned around the world. Ours is a diversified region. Various civilizations have assimilated and interacted with one another under the influence of different cultures, which affords and important cultural foundation for the people China ASEAN countries to learn from and complement one another. We should draw upon the experience of other regions in development and welcome a constructive role by non-regional countries in the development and stability of the region. At the same time, these, non-regional countries should respect the diversity of the region and do more to facilitate regional development and stability. The China ASEAN community of shared destiny is closely linked with the ASEAN community and the East Asia community. The two sides need to bring out their respective strengths to realize diversity, harmony, inclusiveness and common progress for the benefit of the people of the region and beyond. A more closely knit China-ASEAN common destiny conforms to the trend of the times for seeking peace, development, cooperation and mutual benefit, and meets the common interests of the people of Asia and the world, hence enjoying a broad space and huge potential of growth.

Ladies and Gentlemen: Dear Friends, Since the founding of the People's Republic of China over 60 years ago, in particular the launch of reform and opening-up over 30 years ago, China has blazed a successful path of development and made tremendous progress. China has laid out a strategic plan and set clear goals for its future development, namely, to double its 2010 GDP and per capita income of its urban and rural residents and finish the building of a moderately prosperous society in all respects by 2020; and turn China into a modern socialist country that is prosperous, strong, democratic, culturally advanced and harmonious and realize the great renewal of the Chinese nation by the middle of this century. This is a dream that has long been cherished by the Chinese nation and people. It is also a prerequisite for China to make even greater contribution to mankind. As an ancient Chinese maxim goes, "only with high ambition and hard work can one make great achievements." We have the confidence, conditions and capabilities to attain our goals. Having said that, we are soberly aware that China remains the largest developing country in the world. We still face many difficulties and challenges on the way ahead. For all the Chinese people to enjoy a happy life, we have to make unrelenting efforts for a long time to come. We will firmly stay on the course of reform and opening-up, adhere to the path of socialism with Chinese characteristics, focus on managing our own affairs well, press ahead with modernization and improve people's wellbeing. China cannot achieve development in isolation from the world, and the world also needs China for development. China is fully committed to the path of peaceful development, the independent foreign policy of peace and the opening-up strategy for win-win results. A stronger China will add to the force for world peace and the positive energy for friendship, and will present development opportunities to Asia and the world, rather than posing a threat. China will continue to share opportunities for economic and social development with AESAN, Asia and the world.

Ladies and Gentlemen: Dear Friends, The Chinese people are working hard to realize the Chinese dream for the great renewal of the Chinese nation. And here, the Indonesian people are vigorously implementing their overall economic development plan for the rise of Indonesian nation. To realize our respective dreams, it is all the more necessary for both sides to understand, support and cooperate with each other, and for more people of vision in both countries to get involved and make effective efforts to this end.

In this connection, I recall the song Hening(Silence) composed by President Yudhoyono. In October 2006, he came to Guangxi, China for the commemorative summit marking the 15th anniversary of China-ASEAN dialogue relations. On the Lijiang River, President Yudhoyono was overwhelmed by inspiration and wrote down these beautiful lyrics. "The beautiful days I spend with my friends have kept recurring in my life." The mountains and rivers in China deeply touched President Yudhoyono and reminded him of his childhood and hometown. This shows just how strong the bond and affinity are between our two peoples.

Amity between people holds the key to good relations between nations. It is through the efforts of these envoys of friendship who have built bridges of friendship and opened windows to sincere understanding that the friendship between our two peoples has been everlasting and has grown stronger and more robust as time goes by. Young people are full of dynamism and dreams. When the young prosper and are strong, the country will prosper and be strong. Young people represent the future and hope for exchanges between the two countries. President Yudhoyono and I have agreed that the two countries will expand and deepen cultural and people-to-people exchanges. In the next five years, each side will send 100 young people to visit the other every year, and China will provide 1,000 scholarships to Indonesia.

I am convinced that with more and more young people involved in the building of friendship between the two countries, China-Indonesia friendship will flourish and pass on from generation to generation.
Ladies and Gentlemen:

Dear Friends,

China and Indonesia have a combined population of 1.6 billion. As long as our two peoples work hand in hand with one heart and one mind, we will pool the huge strength of one fourth of mankind and be able to create new miracles in the history of human development. Let our two peoples join hands, write a new chapter in growing our bilateral relations, work for a bright future for the China-ASEAN community of shared destiny, and make greater contribution to the lofty cause of world peace and development.

Terima Kasih!(Thank you!)

Appendix "J"

President Xi Jinping Delivers Important Speech and Proposes to Build a Silk Road Economic Belt with Central Asian Countries

2013/09/07

Source :Ministry of Foreign Affairs of the People's Republic of China-
http://www.fmprc.gov.cn/mfa_eng/topics_665678/xjpfwzysies
gjtfhshzzf h_665686/t1076334.shtml

On Sept. 7, 2013, President Xi Jinping made a speech titled "Promote People-to-People Friendship and Create a Better Future" at Kazakhstan's Nazarbayev University. He spoke highly of the traditional friendship between China and Kazakhstan, and gave a comprehensive elaboration of China's policy of good-neighbourly and friendly cooperation toward countries in Central Asia. He proposed to join hands building a Silk Road economic belt with innovative cooperation mode and to make it a grand cause benefiting people in regional countries along the route.

Around 10:30 a.m. local time, Xi Jinping, accompanied by President Nursultan Nazarbayev of Kazakhstan, stepped into the conference hall. Amid warm applause, Xi Jinping made an important speech.

Xi Jinping expressed that more than 2,100 years ago, during China's Western Han Dynasty (206 BC-AD 24), imperial envoy Zhang Qian was sent to Central Asia twice to open the door to friendly contacts between China and Central Asian countries as well as the transcontinental Silk Road linking East and West, Asia and Europe. Kazakhstan, as a major stop along the ancient Silk Road, has made important contributions to the exchanges and cooperation between different nationalities and cultures. People in regional countries created the history of friendship along the ancient Silk Road through the ages.

Xi Jinping pointed out that the 2,000-plus-year history of exchanges had proved that countries with differences in race, belief and cultural background can absolutely share peace and development as long as they persist in unity and mutual trust, equality and mutual benefit, mutual tolerance and learning from each other, as well as cooperation and win-win outcomes.

Xi underscored that over the 20-plus years, the ancient Silk Road is becoming full of new vitality with the rapid development of China's relations with Asian and European countries. It is a foreign-policy priority for China to develop the friendly cooperative relations with the Central

Asian countries. We hope to work with Central Asian countries to unceasingly enhance mutual trust, to consolidate friendship, to strengthen cooperation, so as to push forward the common development and prosperity, and work for the happiness and well-being of the people in the regional countries.

Xi Jinping raised the following proposals: to uphold the friendship from generation to generation and to be harmonious good neighbours for each other. China respects the development path as well as the domestic and foreign policies Central Asian people have independently chosen for themselves. China will never intervene in internal affairs of Central Asian countries, seek leadership in regional affairs, or operate sphere of influence. To strengthen mutual support and to be good friends with sincerity and mutual trust. On the issues concerning the major core interests, including the state sovereignty, territorial integrity, security and stability, we should firmly support each other and make joint efforts to crack down on the "three evil forces" of terrorism, extremism and separatism, as well as drug trafficking, transnational organized crime. To vigorously strengthen the practical cooperation and to be good partners with mutual benefit and win-win opportunities. We should turn the advantage of political relations, the geographical advantage, and the economic complementary advantage into advantages for practical cooperation and for sustainable growth, so as to build a community of interests. We should create new brilliance with a more open mind and a broader vision to expand regional cooperation. By strengthening the cooperation between the Shanghai Cooperation Organization and the Eurasian Economic Community, we can gain a greater space for development.

Xi Jinping proposed that in order to make the economic ties closer, mutual cooperation deeper and space of development broader between the Eurasian countries, we can innovate the mode of cooperation and jointly build the "Silk Road Economic Belt" step by step to gradually form overall regional cooperation. First, to strengthen policy communication. Countries in the region can communicate with each other on economic development strategies, and make plans and measures for regional cooperation through consultations. Second, to improve road connectivity. To open up the transportation channel from the Pacific to the Baltic Sea and to gradually form a transportation network that connects East Asia, West Asia, and South Asia. Third, to promote trade facilitation. All the parties should discuss the issues concerning trade and investment facilitation and make appropriate arrangements. Fourth, to enhance monetary circulation. All the parties should promote the realization of exchange and settlement of local currency, increase the ability to fend off financial risks and make the region more economically competitive in the world. Fifth, to strengthen people-to-people exchanges. All the parties should strengthen the friendly exchanges between their peoples to promote understanding and friendship with each other.

Xi Jinping finally said that China and Kazakhstan are friendly neighbours as close as lips and teeth. A 1,700-plus-kilometer common border, more than 2,000 years of exchanges and broad common interests, bind us together and open up broad prospects for the development of relations between the two countries. Youth is the future of the nation, as well as the major force of the friendship between the people in the two countries. I believe, the young people of the two countries will become the messenger of China-Kazakhstan friendship and contribute their youth and strength to the development of bilateral comprehensive strategic partnership. Let us join hands to carry forward the traditional friendship and create a better future.

Xi Jinping also answered questions from students. When answering questions on environmental protection, Xi Jinping stressed that the construction of ecological civilization is about not only the well-being of the people, but also the future development of the nation. China must take a new path of development for the realization of industrialization, urbanization, informatization, and modernization of agriculture. China clearly puts the protection of the ecological environment in a more prominent position. We need not only economic growth but also good ecological environment, and we prefer good ecological environment rather than economic growth. In fact, good ecological environment itself is a valuable wealth. We must not pursue economic development at the expense of ecological environment. We have put forward a strategic task of the construction of ecological civilization and the building of a more beautiful China with blue sky, green space, and clean water for future generations.

Nazarbayev said in his speech that Kazakhstan and China are good neighbours, good friends and good partners. The bilateral relations have made considerable progress. The Kazakh side thanked for China's support and help, and believed President Xi Jinping's visit would surely promote bilateral mutually beneficial cooperation, and bring the Kazakhstan-China comprehensive strategic partnership to a new high. The Kazakh side fully agreed with the strategic vision of building the "Silk Road Economic Belt" proposed by President Xi Jinping. Kazakhstan is willing to strengthen economic, transportation, people-to-people and cultural connectivity with

China, to jointly build a new Silk Road.

Xi Jinping as well took over from Nazarbayev the certificate of honorary professor granted by Nazarbayev University.

Xi Jinping, accompanied by Nazarbayev, also visited the campus model and engineering laboratory of the university.

Wang Huning, Li Zhanshu, Yang Jiechi and others were present. Officials from Kazakhstan, and foreign diplomats in Kazakhstan also attended the lecture.

Appendix "K"
Vision and Actions on Jointly Building Silk Road Economic Belt and 21st-Century Maritime Silk Road

Issued by the National Development and Reform Commission, Ministry of Foreign Affairs, and Ministry of Commerce of the People's Republic of China, with State Council authorization
March 2015
First Edition 2015

Preface
I.   Background
II.   Principles
III. Framework
IV. Cooperation Priorities
V.   Cooperation Mechanisms
VI. China's Regions in Pursuing Opening-Up
VII. China in Action
VIII. Embracing a Brighter Future Together

Preface

More than two millennia ago the diligent and courageous people of Eurasia explored and opened up several routes of trade and cultural exchanges that linked the major civilizations of Asia, Europe and Africa, collectively called the Silk Road by later generations. For thousands of years, the Silk Road Spirit – "peace and cooperation, openness and inclusiveness, mutual learning and mutual benefit" – has been passed from generation to generation, promoted the progress of human civilization, and contributed greatly to the prosperity and development of the countries along the Silk Road. Symbolizing communication and cooperation between the East and the West, the Silk Road Spirit is a historic and cultural heritage shared by all countries around the world.

In the 21st century, a new era marked by the theme of peace, development, cooperation and mutual benefit, it is all the more important for us to carry on the Silk Road Spirit in face of the weak recovery of the global economy, and complex international and regional situations.

When Chinese President Xi Jinping visited Central Asia and Southeast Asia in September and October of 2013, he raised the initiative of jointly building the Silk Road Economic Belt and the 21st-Century Maritime Silk Road (hereinafter referred to as the Belt and Road), which have attracted close attention from all over the world. At the China-ASEAN Expo in 2013, Chinese Premier Li Keqiang emphasized the need to build the Maritime Silk Road oriented towards ASEAN, and to create strategic propellers for hinterland development. Accelerating the building of the Belt and Road can help promote the economic prosperity of the countries along the Belt and Road and regional economic cooperation, strengthen exchanges and mutual learning between different civilizations, and promote world peace and development. It is a great undertaking that will benefit people around the world.

The Belt and Road Initiative is a systematic project, which should be jointly built through consultation to meet the interests of all, and efforts should be made to integrate the development strategies of the countries along the Belt and Road. The Chinese government has drafted and published the Vision and Actions on Jointly Building Silk Road Economic Belt and 21st-Century Maritime Silk Road to promote the implementation of the Initiative, instill vigor and vitality into the ancient Silk Road, connect Asian, European and African countries more closely and promote mutually beneficial cooperation to a new high and in new forms.

I. Background

Complex and profound changes are taking place in the world. The underlying impact of the international financial crisis keeps emerging; the world economy is recovering slowly, and global development is uneven; the international trade and investment landscape and rules for multilateral trade and investment are undergoing major adjustments; and countries still face big challenges to their development.

The initiative to jointly build the Belt and Road, embracing the trend towards a multipolar world, economic globalization, cultural diversity and greater IT application, is designed to uphold the global free trade regime and the open world economy in the spirit of open regional cooperation. It is aimed at promoting orderly and free flow of economic factors, highly efficient allocation of resources and deep integration of markets; encouraging the countries along the Belt and Road to achieve economic policy coordination and carry out broader and more in-depth regional cooperation of higher standards; and jointly creating an open, inclusive and balanced regional economic cooperation architecture that benefits all. Jointly building the Belt and Road is in the interests of the world community. Reflecting the common ideals and pursuit of human societies, it is a positive endeavor to seek new models of international cooperation and global governance, and will inject new positive energy into world peace and development.

The Belt and Road Initiative aims to promote the connectivity of Asian, European and African continents and their adjacent seas, establish and strengthen partnerships among the countries along the Belt and Road, set up all-dimensional, multi-tiered and composite connectivity networks, and realize diversified, independent, balanced and sustainable development in these countries. The connectivity projects of the Initiative will help align and coordinate the development strategies of the countries along the Belt and Road, tap market potential in this region, promote investment and consumption, create demands and job opportunities, enhance people-to people and cultural exchanges, and mutual learning among the peoples of the relevant countries, and enable them to understand, trust and respect each other and live in harmony, peace and prosperity.

China's economy is closely connected with the world economy. China will stay committed to the basic policy of opening-up, build a new pattern of all-round opening-up, and integrate itself deeper into the world economic system. The Initiative will enable China to further expand and deepen its opening-up, and to strengthen its mutually beneficial cooperation with countries in Asia, Europe and Africa and the rest of the world. China is committed to shouldering more responsibilities and obligations within its capabilities, and making greater contributions to the peace and development of mankind.

II. Principles

The Belt and Road Initiative is in line with the purposes and principles of the UN Charter. It upholds the Five Principles of Peaceful Coexistence: mutual respect for each other's sovereignty and territorial integrity, mutual non-aggression, mutual non-interference in each other's internal affairs, equality and mutual benefit, and peaceful coexistence.

The Initiative is open for cooperation. It covers, but is not limited to, the area of the ancient Silk Road. It is open to all countries, and international and regional organizations for engagement, so that the results of the concerted efforts will benefit wider areas.

The Initiative is harmonious and inclusive. It advocates tolerance among civilizations, respects the paths and modes of development chosen by different countries, and supports dialogues among different civilizations on the principles of seeking common ground while shelving differences and drawing on each other's strengths, so that all countries can coexist in peace for common prosperity.

The Initiative follows market operation. It will abide by market rules and international norms, give play to the decisive role of the market in resource allocation and the primary role of enterprises, and let the governments perform their due functions.

The Initiative seeks mutual benefit. It accommodates the interests and concerns of all parties involved, and seeks a conjunction of interests and the "biggest common denominator" for cooperation so as to give full play to the wisdom and creativity, strengths and potentials of all parties.

III. Framework

The Belt and Road Initiative is a way for win-win cooperation that promotes common development and prosperity and a road towards peace and friendship by enhancing mutual understanding and trust, and strengthening all-round exchanges. The Chinese government advocates peace and cooperation, openness and inclusiveness, mutual learning and mutual benefit. It promotes practical cooperation in all fields, and works to build a community of shared interests, destiny and responsibility featuring mutual political trust, economic integration and cultural inclusiveness.

The Belt and Road run through the continents of Asia, Europe and Africa, connecting the vibrant East Asia economic circle at one end and developed European economic circle at the other, and encompassing countries with huge potential for economic development. The Silk Road Economic Belt focuses on bringing together China, Central Asia, Russia and Europe (the Baltic); linking China with the Persian Gulf and the Mediterranean Sea through Central Asia and West Asia; and connecting China with Southeast Asia, South Asia and the Indian Ocean. The 21stCentury Maritime Silk Road is designed to go from China's coast to Europe through the South China Sea and the Indian Ocean in one route, and from China's coast through the South China Sea to the South Pacific in the other.

On land, the Initiative will focus on jointly building a new Eurasian Land Bridge and developing China-Mongolia-Russia, China-Central Asia West Asia and China-Indochina Peninsula economic corridors by taking advantage of international transport routes, relying on core cities along the Belt and Road and using key economic industrial parks as cooperation platforms. At sea, the Initiative will focus on jointly building smooth, secure and efficient transport routes connecting major sea ports along the Belt and Road. The China-Pakistan Economic Corridor and the Bangladesh-China India-Myanmar Economic Corridor are closely related to the Belt and Road Initiative, and therefore require closer cooperation and greater progress.

The Initiative is an ambitious economic vision of the opening-up of and cooperation among the countries along the Belt and Road. Countries should work in concert and move towards the objectives of mutual benefit and common security. To be specific, they need to improve the region's infrastructure, and put in place a secure and efficient network of land, sea and air passages, lifting their connectivity to a higher level; further enhance trade and investment facilitation, establish a network of free trade areas that meet high standards, maintain closer economic ties, and deepen political trust; enhance cultural exchanges; encourage different civilizations to learn from each other and flourish together; and promote mutual understanding, peace and friendship among people of all countries.

IV. Cooperation Priorities

Countries along the Belt and Road have their own resource advantages and their economies are mutually complementary. Therefore, there is a great potential and space for cooperation. They should promote policy coordination, facilities connectivity, unimpeded trade, financial integration and people-to-people bonds as their five major goals, and strengthen cooperation in the following key areas:

Policy coordination

Enhancing policy coordination is an important guarantee for implementing the Initiative. We should promote intergovernmental cooperation, build a multi-level intergovernmental macro policy exchange and communication mechanism, expand shared interests, enhance mutual political trust, and reach new cooperation consensus. Countries along the Belt and Road may fully coordinate their economic development strategies and policies, work out plans and measures for regional cooperation, negotiate to solve cooperation-related issues, and jointly provide policy support for the implementation of practical cooperation and large-scale projects.

Facilities connectivity

Facilities connectivity is a priority area for implementing the Initiative. On the basis of respecting each other's sovereignty and security concerns, countries along the Belt and Road should improve the connectivity of their infrastructure construction plans and technical standard systems, jointly push forward the construction of international trunk passageways, and form an infrastructure network connecting all sub-regions in Asia, and between Asia, Europe and Africa step by step. At the same time, efforts should be made to promote green and low-carbon infrastructure construction and operation management, taking into full account the impact of climate change on the construction.

With regard to transport infrastructure construction, we should focus on the key passageways, junctions and projects, and give priority to linking up unconnected road sections, removing transport bottlenecks, advancing road safety facilities and traffic management facilities and equipment, and improving road network connectivity. We should build a unified coordination mechanism for whole-course transportation, increase connectivity of customs clearance, reloading and multimodal transport between countries, and gradually formulate compatible and standard transport rules, so as to realize international transport facilitation. We should push forward port infrastructure construction, build smooth land water transportation channels, and advance port cooperation; increase sea routes and the number of voyages, and enhance information technology cooperation in maritime logistics. We should expand and build platforms and mechanisms for comprehensive civil aviation cooperation, and quicken our pace in improving aviation infrastructure.

We should promote cooperation in the connectivity of energy infrastructure, work in concert to ensure the security of oil and gas pipelines and other transport routes, build cross-border power supply networks and power-transmission routes, and cooperate in regional power grid upgrading and transformation.

We should jointly advance the construction of cross-border optical cables and other communications trunk line networks, improve international communications connectivity, and create an Information Silk Road. We should build bilateral cross-border optical cable networks at a quicker pace, plan transcontinental submarine optical cable projects, and improve spatial (satellite) information passageways to expand information exchanges and cooperation.

Unimpeded trade

Investment and trade cooperation is a major task in building the Belt and Road. We should strive to improve investment and trade facilitation, and remove investment and trade barriers for the creation of a sound business environment within the region and in all related countries. We will discuss with countries and regions along the Belt and Road on opening free trade areas so as to unleash the potential for expanded cooperation.

Countries along the Belt and Road should enhance customs cooperation such as information exchange, mutual recognition of regulations, and mutual assistance in law enforcement; improve bilateral and multilateral cooperation in the fields of inspection and quarantine, certification and accreditation, standard measurement, and statistical information; and work to ensure that the WTO Trade Facilitation Agreement takes effect and is implemented. We should improve the customs clearance facilities of border ports, establish a "single-window" in border ports, reduce customs clearance costs, and improve customs clearance capability. We should increase cooperation in supply chain safety and convenience, improve the coordination of cross-border supervision procedures, promote online checking of inspection and quarantine certificates, and facilitate mutual recognition of Authorized Economic Operators. We should lower non-tariff barriers, jointly improve the transparency of technical trade measures, and enhance trade liberalization and facilitation.

We should expand trading areas, improve trade structure, explore new growth areas of trade, and promote trade balance. We should make innovations in our forms of trade, and develop cross-border e-commerce and other modern business models. A service trade support system should be set up to consolidate and expand conventional trade, and efforts to develop modern service trade should be strengthened. We should integrate investment and trade, and promote trade through investment.

We should speed up investment facilitation, eliminate investment barriers, and push forward negotiations on bilateral investment protection agreements and double taxation avoidance agreements to protect the lawful rights and interests of investors.

We should expand mutual investment areas, deepen cooperation in agriculture, forestry, animal husbandry and fisheries, agricultural machinery manufacturing and farm produce processing, and promote cooperation in marine-product farming, deep-sea fishing, aquatic product processing, seawater desalination, marine biopharmacy, ocean engineering technology, environmental protection industries, marine tourism and other fields. We should increase cooperation in the exploration and development of coal, oil, gas, metal minerals and other conventional energy sources; advance cooperation in hydropower, nuclear power, wind power, solar power and other clean, renewable energy sources; and promote cooperation in the processing and conversion of energy and resources at or near places where they are exploited, so as to create an integrated industrial chain of energy and resource cooperation. We should enhance cooperation in deep processing technology, equipment and engineering services in the fields of energy and resources.

We should push forward cooperation in emerging industries. In accordance with the principles of mutual complementarity and mutual benefit, we should promote in-depth cooperation with other countries along the Belt and Road in new-generation information technology, biotechnology, new energy technology, new materials and other emerging industries, and establish entrepreneurial and investment cooperation mechanisms.

We should improve the division of labor and distribution of industrial chains by encouraging the entire industrial chain and related industries to develop in concert; establish R&D, production and marketing systems; and improve industrial supporting capacity and the overall competitiveness of regional industries. We should increase the openness of our service industry to each other to accelerate the development of regional service industries. We should explore a new mode of investment cooperation, working together to build all forms of industrial parks such as overseas economic and trade cooperation zones and cross-border economic cooperation zones, and promote industrial cluster development. We should promote ecological progress in conducting investment and trade, increase cooperation in conserving eco-environment, protecting biodiversity, and tackling climate change, and join hands to make the Silk Road an environment-friendly one.

We welcome companies from all countries to invest in China, and encourage Chinese enterprises to participate in infrastructure construction in other countries along the Belt and Road, and make industrial investments there. We support localized operation and management of Chinese companies to boost the local economy, increase local employment, improve local livelihood, and take social responsibilities in protecting local biodiversity and eco-environment.

Financial integration

Financial integration is an important underpinning for implementing the Belt and Road Initiative. We should deepen financial cooperation, and make more efforts in building a currency stability system, investment and financing system and credit information system in Asia. We should expand the scope and scale of bilateral currency swap and settlement with other countries along the Belt and Road, open and develop the bond market in Asia, make joint efforts to establish the Asian Infrastructure Investment Bank and BRICS New Development Bank, conduct negotiation among related parties on establishing Shanghai Cooperation Organization (SCO) financing institution, and set up and put into operation the Silk Road Fund as early as possible. We should strengthen practical cooperation of China ASEAN Interbank Association and SCO Interbank Association, and carry out multilateral financial cooperation in the form of syndicated loans and bank credit. We will support the efforts of governments of the countries along the Belt and Road and their companies and financial institutions with good credit-rating to issue Renminbi bonds in China. Qualified Chinese financial institutions and companies are encouraged to issue bonds in both Renminbi and foreign currencies outside China, and use the funds thus collected in countries along the Belt and Road.

We should strengthen financial regulation cooperation, encourage the signing of MOUs on cooperation in bilateral financial regulation, and establish an efficient regulation coordination mechanism in the region. We should improve the system of risk response and crisis management, build a regional financial risk early-warning system, and create an exchange and cooperation mechanism of addressing cross-border risks and crisis. We should increase cross-border exchange and cooperation between credit investigation regulators, credit investigation institutions and credit rating institutions. We should give full play to the role of the Silk Road Fund and that of sovereign wealth funds of countries along the Belt and Road, and encourage commercial equity investment funds and private funds to participate in the construction of key projects of the Initiative.

People-to-people bond

People-to-people bond provides the public support for implementing the Initiative. We should carry forward the spirit of friendly cooperation of the Silk Road by promoting extensive cultural and academic exchanges, personnel exchanges and cooperation, media cooperation, youth and women exchanges and volunteer services, so as to win public support for deepening bilateral and multilateral cooperation.

We should send more students to each other's countries, and promote cooperation in jointly running schools. China provides 10,000 government scholarships to the countries along the Belt and Road every year. We should hold culture years, arts festivals, film festivals, TV weeks and book fairs in each other's countries; cooperate on the production and translation of fine films, radio and TV programs; and jointly apply for and protect

World Cultural Heritage sites. We should also increase personnel exchange and cooperation between countries along the Belt and Road. We should enhance cooperation in and expand the scale of tourism; hold tourism promotion weeks and publicity months in each other's countries; jointly create competitive international tourist routes and products with Silk Road features; and make it more convenient to apply for tourist visa in countries along the Belt and Road. We should push forward cooperation on the 21st-Century Maritime Silk Road cruise tourism program. We should carry out sports exchanges and support countries along the Belt and Road in their bid for hosting major international sports events.

We should strengthen cooperation with neighboring countries on epidemic information sharing, the exchange of prevention and treatment technologies and the training of medical professionals, and improve our capability to jointly address public health emergencies. We will provide medical assistance and emergency medical aid to relevant countries, and carry out practical cooperation in maternal and child health, disability rehabilitation, and major infectious diseases including AIDS, tuberculosis and malaria. We will also expand cooperation on traditional medicine.

We should increase our cooperation in science and technology, establish joint labs (or research centers), international technology transfer centers and maritime cooperation centers, promote sci-tech personnel exchanges, cooperate in tackling key sci-tech problems, and work together to improve sci-tech innovation capability.

We should integrate existing resources to expand and advance practical cooperation between countries along the Belt and Road on youth employment, entrepreneurship training, vocational skill development, social security management, public administration and management and in other areas of common interest.

We should give full play to the bridging role of communication between political parties and parliaments, and promote friendly exchanges between legislative bodies, major political parties and political organizations of countries along the Belt and Road. We should carry out exchanges and cooperation among cities, encourage major cities in these countries to become sister cities, focus on promoting practical cooperation, particularly cultural and people-to-people exchanges, and create more lively examples of cooperation. We welcome the think tanks in the countries along the Belt and Road to jointly conduct research and hold forums.

We should increase exchanges and cooperation between nongovernmental organizations of countries along the Belt and Road, organize public interest activities concerning education, health care, poverty reduction, biodiversity and ecological protection for the benefit of the general public, and improve the production and living conditions of poverty-stricken areas along the Belt and Road. We should enhance international exchanges and cooperation on culture and media, and leverage the positive role of the Internet and new media tools to foster harmonious and friendly cultural environment and public opinion.

V. Cooperation Mechanisms

The world economic integration is accelerating and regional cooperation is on the upswing. China will take full advantage of the existing bilateral and multilateral cooperation mechanisms to push forward the building of the Belt and Road and to promote the development of regional cooperation.

We should strengthen bilateral cooperation, and promote comprehensive development of bilateral relations through multi-level and multi-channel communication and consultation. We should encourage the signing of cooperation MOUs or plans, and develop a number of bilateral cooperation pilot projects. We should establish and improve bilateral joint working mechanisms, and draw up implementation plans and roadmaps for advancing the Belt and Road Initiative. In addition, we should give full play to the existing bilateral mechanisms such as joint committee, mixed committee, coordinating committee, steering committee and management committee to coordinate and promote the implementation of cooperation projects.

We should enhance the role of multilateral cooperation mechanisms, make full use of existing mechanisms such as the Shanghai Cooperation Organization (SCO), ASEAN Plus China (10+1), Asia-Pacific Economic Cooperation (APEC), Asia-Europe Meeting (ASEM), Asia Cooperation Dialogue (ACD), Conference on Interaction and Confidence-Building Measures in Asia (CICA), China-Arab States Cooperation Forum (CASCF), China-Gulf Cooperation Council Strategic Dialogue, Greater Mekong

Subregion (GMS) Economic Cooperation, and Central Asia Regional Economic Cooperation (CAREC) to strengthen communication with relevant countries, and attract more countries and regions to participate in the Belt and Road Initiative.

We should continue to encourage the constructive role of the international forums and exhibitions at regional and sub-regional levels hosted by countries along the Belt and Road, as well as such platforms as Boao Forum for Asia, China-ASEAN Expo, China-Eurasia Expo, Euro Asia Economic Forum, China International Fair for Investment and Trade, China-South Asia Expo, China-Arab States Expo, Western China International Fair, China-Russia Expo, and Qianhai Cooperation Forum. We should support the local authorities and general public of countries along the Belt and Road to explore the historical and cultural heritage of the Belt and Road, jointly hold investment, trade and cultural exchange activities, and ensure the success of the Silk Road (Dunhuang) International Culture Expo, Silk Road International Film Festival and Silk Road International Book Fair. We propose to set up an international summit forum on the Belt and Road Initiative.

VI. China's Regions in Pursuing Opening-Up

In advancing the Belt and Road Initiative, China will fully leverage the comparative advantages of its various regions, adopt a proactive strategy of further opening-up, strengthen interaction and cooperation among the eastern, western and central regions, and comprehensively improve the openness of the Chinese economy.

Northwestern and northeastern regions. We should make good use of Xinjiang's geographic advantages and its role as a window of westward opening-up to deepen communication and cooperation with Central, South and West Asian countries, make it a key transportation, trade, logistics, culture, science and education center, and a core area on the Silk Road Economic Belt. We should give full scope to the economic and cultural strengths of Shaanxi and Gansu provinces and the ethnic and cultural advantages of the Ningxia Hui Autonomous Region and Qinghai Province, build Xi'an into a new focus of reform and opening-up in China's interior, speed up the development and opening-up of cities such as Lanzhou and Xining, and advance the building of the Ningxia Inland Opening-up Pilot Economic Zone with the goal of creating strategic channels, trade and logistics hubs and key bases for industrial and cultural exchanges opening to Central, South and West Asian countries. We should give full play to Inner Mongolia's proximity to Mongolia and Russia, improve the railway links connecting Heilongjiang Province with Russia and the regional railway network, strengthen cooperation between China's Heilongjiang, Jilin and Liaoning provinces and Russia's Far East region on sea-land multi-modal transport, and advance the construction of an Eurasian high-speed transport corridor linking Beijing and Moscow with the goal of building key windows opening to the north.

Southwestern region. We should give full play to the unique advantage of Guangxi Zhuang Autonomous Region as a neighbor of ASEAN countries, speed up the opening-up and development of the Beibu Gulf Economic Zone and the Pearl River-Xijiang Economic Zone, build an international corridor opening to the ASEAN region, create new strategic anchors for the opening-up and development of the southwest and midsouth regions of China, and form an important gateway connecting the Silk Road Economic Belt and the 21st-Century Maritime Silk Road. We should make good use of the geographic advantage of Yunnan Province, advance the construction of an international transport corridor connecting China with neighboring countries, develop a new highlight of economic cooperation in the Greater Mekong Sub-region, and make the region a pivot of China's opening-up to South and Southeast Asia. We should promote the border trade and tourism and culture cooperation between Tibet Autonomous Region and neighboring countries such as Nepal.

Coastal regions, and Hong Kong, Macao and Taiwan. We should leverage the strengths of the Yangtze River Delta, Pearl River Delta, west coast of the Taiwan Straits, Bohai Rim, and other areas with economic zones boasting a high level of openness, robust economic strengths and strong catalytic role, speed up the development of the China (Shanghai) Pilot Free Trade Zone, and support Fujian Province in becoming a core area of the 21st-Century Maritime Silk Road. We should give full scope to the role of Qianhai (Shenzhen), Nansha (Guangzhou), Hengqin (Zhuhai) and Pingtan (Fujian) in opening-up and cooperation, deepen their cooperation with Hong Kong, Macao and Taiwan, and help to build the Guangdong-Hong Kong-Macao Big Bay Area. We should promote the development of the Zhejiang Marine Economy Development Demonstration Zone, Fujian Marine Economic Pilot Zone and Zhoushan Archipelago New Area, and further open Hainan Province as an international tourism island. We should strengthen the port construction of coastal cities such as Shanghai, Tianjin, Ningbo-Zhoushan, Guangzhou, Shenzhen, Zhanjiang, Shantou, Qingdao, Yantai, Dalian, Fuzhou, Xiamen, Quanzhou, Haikou and Sanya, and strengthen the functions of international hub airports such as Shanghai and Guangzhou. We should use opening-up to motivate these areas to carry out deeper reform, create new systems and mechanisms of open economy, step up scientific and technological innovation, develop new advantages for participating in and leading international cooperation and competition, and become the pace-setter and main force in the Belt and Road Initiative, particularly the building of the 21st-Century Maritime Silk Road. We should leverage the unique role of overseas Chinese and the Hong Kong and Macao Special Administrative Regions, and encourage them to participate in and contribute to the Belt and Road Initiative. We should also make proper arrangements for the Taiwan region to be part of this effort.

Inland regions. We should make use of the advantages of inland regions, including a vast landmass, rich human resources and a strong industrial foundation, focus on such key regions as the city clusters along the middle reaches of the Yangtze River, around Chengdu and Chongqing, in central Henan Province, around Hohhot, Baotou, Erdos and Yulin, and around Harbin and Changchun to propel regional interaction and cooperation and industrial concentration. We should build Chongqing into an important pivot for developing and opening up the western region, and make Chengdu, Zhengzhou, Wuhan, Changsha, Nanchang and Hefei leading areas of opening-up in the inland regions. We should accelerate cooperation between regions on the upper and middle reaches of the Yangtze River and their counterparts along Russia's Volga River. We should set up coordination mechanisms in terms of railway transport and port customs clearance for the China-Europe corridor, cultivate the brand of "China-Europe freight trains," and construct a cross-border transport corridor connecting the eastern, central and western regions. We should support inland cities such as Zhengzhou and Xi'an in building airports and international land ports, strengthen customs clearance cooperation between inland ports and ports in the coastal and border regions, and launch pilot ecommerce services for cross-border trade. We should optimize the layout of special customs oversight areas, develop new models of processing trade, and deepen industrial cooperation with countries along the Belt and Road.

VII. China in Action

For more than a year, the Chinese government has been actively promoting the building of the Belt and Road, enhancing communication and consultation and advancing practical cooperation with countries along the Belt and Road, and introduced a series of policies and measures for early outcomes.

High-level guidance and facilitation. President Xi Jinping and Premier Li Keqiang have visited over 20 countries, attended the Dialogue on Strengthening Connectivity Partnership and the sixth ministerial conference of the China-Arab States Cooperation Forum, and met with leaders of relevant countries to discuss bilateral relations and regional development issues. They have used these opportunities to explain the rich contents and positive implications of the Belt and Road Initiative, and their efforts have helped bring about a broad consensus on the Belt and Road Initiative.

Signing cooperation framework. China has signed MOUs of cooperation on the joint development of the Belt and Road with some countries, and on regional cooperation and border cooperation and mid- and long-term development plans for economic and trade cooperation with some neighboring countries. It has proposed outlines of regional cooperation plans with some adjacent countries.

Promoting project cooperation. China has enhanced communication and consultation with countries along the Belt and Road, and promoted a number of key cooperation projects in the fields of infrastructure connectivity, industrial investment, resource development, economic and trade cooperation, financial cooperation, cultural exchanges, ecological protection and maritime cooperation where the conditions are right.

Initiative. It will facilitate the establishment of the Asian Infrastructure Investment Bank. China has proposed the Silk Road Fund, and the investment function of the China-Eurasia Economic Cooperation Fund will be reinforced. We will encourage bank card clearing institutions to conduct cross-border clearing operations, and payment institutions to conduct cross-border payment business. We will actively promote investment and trade facilitation, and accelerate the reform of integrated regional customs clearance.

Boosting the role of cooperation platforms. A number of international summits, forums, seminars and expos on the theme of the Belt and Road Initiative have been held, which have played an important role in increasing mutual understanding, reaching consensus and deepening cooperation.

VIII. Embracing a Brighter Future Together

Though proposed by China, the Belt and Road Initiative is a common aspiration of all countries along their routes. China is ready to conduct equal-footed consultation with all countries along the Belt and Road to seize the opportunity provided by the Initiative, promote opening-up, communication and integration among countries in a larger scope, with higher standards and at deeper levels, while giving consideration to the interests and aspirations of all parties. The development of the Belt and Road is open and inclusive, and we welcome the active participation of all countries and international and regional organizations in this Initiative.

The development of the Belt and Road should mainly be conducted through policy communication and objectives coordination. It is a pluralistic and open process of cooperation which can be highly flexible, and does not seek conformity. China will join other countries along the Belt and Road to substantiate and improve the content and mode of the Belt and Road cooperation, work out relevant timetables and roadmaps, and align national development programs and regional cooperation plans. China will work with countries along the Belt and Road to carry out joint research, forums and fairs, personnel training, exchanges and visits under the framework of existing bilateral, multilateral, regional and sub-regional cooperation mechanisms, so that they will gain a better understanding and recognition of the contents, objectives and tasks of the

Belt and Road Initiative.

China will work with countries along the Belt and Road to steadily advance demonstration projects, jointly identify programs that accommodate bilateral and multilateral interests, and accelerate the launching of programs that are agreed upon by parties and ready for implementation, so as to ensure early harvest.

The Belt and Road cooperation features mutual respect and trust, mutual benefit and win-win cooperation, and mutual learning between civilizations. As long as all countries along the Belt and Road make concerted efforts to pursue our common goal, there will be bright prospects for the Silk Road Economic Belt and the 21st-Century Maritime Silk Road, and the people of countries along the Belt and Road can all benefit from this Initiative.

REFERENCES

ASEAN-China Centre (2013) *Speech by Chinese President H.E. Xi Jinping to Indonesian Parliament.*(2 October 2013, Jakarta, Indonesia. October 2,2013). Retrieved from http://www.asean-china-center.org/english/2013-10/03/c_133062675.htm

Boao Forum for Asia (2014) *Speech delivered by H.E. Yang Jiechi , State Councilor of the People's Republic of China at the Session of "Reviving the Silk Road: A Dialogue with Asian Leaders"* at the Boao Forum for Asia Annual Conference 2014.Boao, Hainan, 10 April 2014. Retrieved from http://english.boaoforum.org/ac2014news/13794.jhtml

Boao Forum for Asia (2015) . *Keynote Speech by H.E. Xi Jinping, President of the People's Republic of China, at the Boao Forum for Asia Annual Conference 2015: Towards a Community of Common Destiny and A New Future* for Asia Boao, 28 March 2015. Retrieved from http://english.boaoforum.org/hynew/19353.jhtml

Confucius Headquarters (2014)*Keynote Speech delivered by H.E. Liu Yandong, Vice Premier of P. R. China, Chair of Council of the Confucius Institute Headquarters at the Opening Ceremony of the 9th Confucius Institute Conference : Towards a New Decade of Confucius Institutes (* 2014-12-08 11:41- Confucius Institute Online 京ICP备08002516号)Retrieved from http://conference.chinesecio.com/en/?q=node/119

Hanban. (2010). *What are the features of the Confucius Institute's operation?* December 3, 2013 Retrieved from   English.hanban.org/article/2010-07/02/content_153909.html

Hanban (2008) Confucius Institute Headquarters. 2008 Annual Report

Hanban, Jan. 19th, Thailand—Hanban's representative office in Thailand in conjunction with the Confucius Institute at Chulalongkorn University held the "Thailand Confucius Institutes & Confucius Classrooms Seminar" and 2009 retrospective meeting.

Meng, Li (2016) *13th "Chinese Bridge-Diamond Crown Jewel" International Chinese Language Contest held in Bangkok.* Hanban: Confucius Institute of Maritime Silk Road. Retrieved from http://english.hanban.org/article/2017-09/13/content_698811.htm

Ministry of Foreign Affairs of the People's Republic of China- Boao (2015) *Forum for Asia Annual Conference 2015: Towards a Community of Common Destiny and A New Future for Asia Boao,* March 28,2015. Retrieved from http://www.fmprc.gov.cn/mfa_eng/wjdt_665385/zyjh_665391/t125 0690.shtml

Ministry of Foreign Affairs of the People's Republic of China(2013) *President Xi Jinping Delivers Important Speech and Proposes to Build a Silk Road Economic Belt with Central Asian Countries* (2013/09/07). Retrieved from http://www.fmprc.gov.cn/mfa_eng/topics_665678/xjpfwzysiesgjtfhs hzzfh_665686/t1076334.shtml

National Development and Reform Commission, Ministry of Foreign Affairs, and Ministry of Commerce of the People's Republic of China, with State Council authorization (2015). *Vision and Actions on Jointly Building Silk Road Economic Belt and 21st-Century Maritime Silk Road,* First Edition .March 20

Phraprommangkalachan (2015) *Confucius Institute of Maritime Silk Road: A Diplomatic Strategy for World Peace and Development.* Amazon : CreateSpace Independent Publishing Platform *Product Website* .Retrieved from https://www.amazon.com/Confucius-Institute-Maritime-Silk-Road/dp/1517486084/ref=tmm_pap_title_0?_encoding=UTF8&qid =&sr

Phraprommangkalachan (2015*) Traimit Educational Model for the First Confucius School in Thailand.* Amazon : CreateSpace Independent Publishing Platform *Product Website.* Retrieved from https://www.amazon.com/Traimit-Educational-Confucius-School-Thailand

Sripatum International University (2017) *Academic Collaboration with the Confucius Institute of Maritime Silk Road*
https://www.spu.ac.th/fac/intl/en/content.php?cid=774

Thailand Maritime Silk Road Confucius Institute (2016) *Agreement on Establishing Maritime Silk Road Confucius Institute Branch Officially Signed*
http://english.hanban.org/article/2016-12/28/content_670033.htm

Yongyou. M (2016) *Thailand: the Confucius Institute reaches its large scale after 10 years* .Guangming Daily Oct. 6, 2016, Page 3 Retrieved from
http://english.hanban.org/article/2016-10/28/content_662117.htm

Phraprommangkalachan

Nationality: Thai

Position: Deputy Supreme Patriarch of Thailand, Deputy Abbot of the Traimit Witthayaram Temple, Chair of the Board of Confucius Institute of Maritime Silk Road and Confucius Classroom at Traimit Wittayalai High School, Thailand

Phraprommangkalachan has been dedicated to the friendship of China and Thailand, educational, and cultural exchange. He has made a unique contribution to Chinese-language teaching for youth in Thailand. In 1999, with the permission of Ministry of Education, he founded the first Chinese language teaching center at Traimit Wittayalai High School at the Traimit Witthayaram Temple. After that he led the efforts in setting up Chinese learning courses at 438 schools in Bangkok. In 2006 he initiated the partnership between Traimit Wittayalai High School and Tianjin Experimental High School to establish the Confucius Classroom at Traimit Wittayalai High School-the world's first Confucius Classroom. In 2015 he worked with Thailand's higher education institutions (such as Dhurakij Pundit University) and Chinese universities such as Tianjin Normal University to found the first Confucius Institute of Maritime Silk Road.

He also supported the efforts of developing 32 volumes of teaching materials titled *Joyful Visit to China*, which have been adopted by more than 200 schools in Thailand to the benefit of hundreds of thousands of Chinese learners. In addition, he gives enormous support for Thailand's native Chinese language teachers to go to China for training programs, and to expand the cohort of the native Chinese-teaching staff. Phraprommangkalachan created the Treasure-Gem King Chinese Bridge Chinese Language Competition which has been held annually for 12 consecutive sessions with a total of 60,000 participants. He was awarded for special contribution by Thailand's Ministry of Education.

In 2015, *Confucius Institute of Maritime Silk Road: A Diplomatic Strategy for World Peace and Development* and *Traimit Educational Model for the First Confucius School in Thailand*, which were compiled and written by him were officially published on Amazon. These books summarize successful practices in operating the Confucius Classroom at Traimit Wittayalai High School for the past decade, shed light on the current situation of Chinese language teaching in Thailand under the 'Road and Belt Initiative' framework, and put forward new approaches and roadmaps.

Phraprommangkalachan was awarded "Confucius Institute Outstanding Contribution Award" for his special contributions at the 6th Confucius Institute Conference. The Confucius Classroom at Traimit Wittayalai High School founded by him was also rated as Confucius Classroom of the Year in 2012 and 2014 respectively.